MW00639854

"Rusty Small has experienced and le(church. As a local church pastor, he r shepherded his own church through the process. He is also a theologian and professor, so he has researched and is able to offer guidance regarding a biblically sound methodology for church revitalization. Furthermore, he now serves in leading our efforts to see a church revitalization movement take place among hundreds of churches in our larger fellowship of churches. I know firsthand that this book is birthed out of a real-world understanding of the need, as well as the opportunity, to see churches not just survive, but thrive!"

—Dr. Brian Autry,
Executive Director, Southern Baptist Convention of Virginia

"Church revitalization is a massive need, and we don't have enough resources to help struggling congregations. Russell Small makes a big contribution to filling the gap with *Church Revitalization: A Pastoral Guide to Church Renewal*. He answers some key questions most revitalizers face and provides a strategic and practical foundation for any leader in a church revitalization scenario."

—Sam Rainer, President, Church Answers

"Over many years of working with churches, I have found that revitalization can be tasking, unprecedented, and overwhelming. Some churches have negative habits, adrift from the biblical mandate, limited resources, and a systemic problem to multiply and mobilize. This book combines the concepts of church revitalization, growth, conflict resolution, and polity into an introductory guidebook to understand the need and navigation for renewal. I wish I had this book when I started, especially during my first 1,000 days. If you are beginning revitalization, you need your Bible in one hand and this book in the other."

—Dr. Gary Moritz, Lead Pastor of City United Church,
SME for Church Revitalization and Renewal, Liberty University,
Director of Baptist Churches of New England for Church Revitalization and Renewal,
Author of *Carry On: Tactical Strategies for Church Revitalization and Renewal*

"Several years ago, I was writing a book on evangelism. A mentor of mine said with profundity, 'Thom, we don't need another book on what evangelism is; we need a book on how evangelism must be done.' I echo his admonition. We don't need another book on what church revitalization is; we need a book on how church revitalization must be done. Now you have the book. It's called *Church Revitalization: A Pastoral Guide to Church Renewal* by Russell Small. Read it. Then do it."

—Thom S. Rainer,
Founder and CEO, Church Answers,
author of *I Am a Christian*

"Helping churches find new life is a continuing challenge for ministry leaders today. This book is an excellent guide for this important task. Practical, workable, spiritual, realistic— all concepts interwoven through these pages. Healthy churches are the primary means for spiritual renewal and stability in communities. If you are a church leader committed to revitalizing your church, this book will help chart your path forward."

—Jeff Iorg, President, Gateway Seminary,
Author of *Leading Major Change in Your Ministry*

"Russell Small's approach moves beyond defining church revitalization; he created a process-driven resource for churches determining their revitalization pathway. Russell graciously walks a church through identifying who they are, where they've been, where they need to go, and who can help them accomplish the task. This much-needed resource provides more than a checklist, but a dialogical approach to solving issues for a congregation in revitalization."
—Kenneth W. Priest,
Founder, Revive This Church Ministries, revivethischurch.com

"Russell (Rusty) Small is an excellent scholar and a faithful pastor. This reality shines throughout this very fine book on church revitalization. It is biblical, theological, and practical. It is well written, and it is structured in such a way that it can serve as a valuable resource to be consulted again and again. This is essential reading for those called to this critically important work."
—Daniel L. Akin,
President, Southeastern Baptist Theological Seminary

"If we say that we love Jesus but show little concern for his church, we have truly deceived ourselves. Rusty Small has labored to produce a resource that screams, 'I love the church!' He embodies our mission here in the John W. Rawlings School of Divinity to come alongside the local church in its quest to fulfill the Great Commission. His insights gained, from diligent research and intentional relationships with pastors, is both convicting and inspiring. The task is hard, but your church will be healthier with these insights."
—Troy W. Temple,
Dean, John W. Rawlings School of Divinity, Liberty University

"I am excited to read Rusty Small's book, *Church Revitalization: A Pastoral Guide to Church Renewal*. Rusty writes, not only from the viewpoint of a state convention leader, but also from the perspective of a pastor who has led his church through revitalization. I plan to use this book to train and to encourage my staff because every chapter addresses critical issues facing revitalization pastors and insights that provide a practical application of biblical wisdom. I am especially enthused about his chapter on 'Managing Conflict, Making Peace.' If you are a revitalization pastor, you need this book."
—William D. Henard,
Adjunct Professor of Church Revitalization, The Southern Baptist Theological Seminary
Author of *Can These Bones Live?* and *ReClaimed Church*
Senior Pastor, First Baptist Church, Athens, TN

"No cookie-cutter approach here, and that's what makes this book worth your time and investment! Dr. Small's book, *Church Revitalization: A Pastoral Guide to Church Renewal*, will cause you to ask the right questions, in order to find the correct solution for your own local church. It understands that no two churches are alike. By focusing on your church's uniqueness in history, community, and pastoral leadership, you can implement a customized strategy plan for long-term success. Forge your own future by following the encouragement and wisdom the author shares here. You'll be glad you did."
—Dr. J. David Jackson,
Replant Specialist, North American Mission Board, SBC
Author of *ReNew: Traveling the Forgotten Path*

CHURCH REVITALIZATION

A PASTORAL GUIDE TO CHURCH RENEWAL

Russell N. Small

KREGEL
MINISTRY

Church Revitalization: A Pastoral Guide to Church Renewal

© 2023 by Russell N. Small

Published by Kregel Ministry, an imprint of Kregel Publications, 2450 Oak Industrial Dr. NE, Grand Rapids, MI 49505-6020.

ISBN 978-0-8254-4753-2

Printed in the United States of America

23 24 25 26 27 / 5 4 3 2 1

*To Liberty Baptist Church, Appomattox,
Virginia, for their graciousness and patience.
To my wife, Melissa, for her support
in ministry and her help editing.
To my two sons, James and Thomas,
I pray the church will be strong for them.*

CONTENTS

INTRODUCTION

The task of church revitalization is necessary today in many churches. Pastors need to be equipped to meet the need of this moment and see the church flourish. Church revitalization is a noble calling and a humbling endeavor. This endeavor requires both dependency upon God and a skill set that is capable of the task. This book attempts to provide an overview of both the theory and practice required for this task. The logic of this book requires an understanding that this book is divided into two major sections.

The first five chapters of the book will provide the ability to assess critical areas in church revitalization. Chapter one will offer the ability to assess where a particular church is in the revitalization process and review skills that the revitalizer will need to embrace to be successful. Chapter two will walk a church leader through the many decisions one must make to clarify the nature of a particular church. Chapter three will review the history of a particular church. A church leader will need to gain a good understanding of what the church has been so that he can understand possible paths for the future. Chapter four will offer an approach to assess the community around the church. Oftentimes, community demographics change, and the spiritual needs of the current community must be understood. Chapter five will assess the overall health of the pastor and offer helpful checkpoints for a pastor to be able to develop a plan for greater health.

The last five chapters will outline a practical approach to implementing church revitalization initiatives. Chapter six will simply review the necessity of a clear, actionable plan. Many things must be done to accomplish revitalization in a church, but these must be prioritized and executed in an orderly fashion. Chapter seven states the necessity of a team. A pastor cannot and should not attempt revitalization alone. Therefore, the logistics of team organization and readiness must be evaluated. Chapter eight reviews the difficulty of execution. Execution is more about emotional resoluteness than strategy. A good strategy must be implemented; the process of implementation is full of stressors. Chapter nine addresses the reality of conflict. Change produces conflict, and conflict that is not managed properly can stop a revitalization effort. Chapter ten discusses future steps in church revitalization after a season of revitalization has occurred. Many churches have been in decline for years, so it typically takes years of sustained effort to see revitalization fully occur. My prayer is for you to read this book with intentionality and prayerfulness, not merely attempting to understand the nature of church revitalization but with a genuine intention to cultivate revitalization in your church context!

CHAPTER 1

WHERE TO START?

Welcome to the journey of church revitalization! What a joy to overview a process for church renewal. This book is not merely a book of tips or quick fixes. The content of this book will need to be processed slowly and implemented strategically. There are unique challenges in every church revitalization situation. Pastors and church leadership will know the specifics of a particular church situation better than anyone else.[1] However, there are key areas of competency required to negotiate church revitalization. Many pastors and church leaders are daunted by the task ahead. Churches often have deeply rooted habits, limited resources, and a lack of

---

1   The intended readership will primarily be in a pastoral role. The content of the book, however, applies most directly to pastors or church leaders who have a primary role in leading a church through revitalization. Therefore, the terms *pastors* and *church leaders* are used throughout the book to denote the group of people who are primary in leading the church revitalization effort. Some sections of the book are more squarely focused on the pastoral office. Other sections of the book are broader in their application to pastors and church leadership because church revitalization is a team effort. Additionally, my personal belief is that the pastoral office is reserved for men, so I will utilize masculine pronouns to refer to pastoral roles throughout this book.

vision and strategy. Church leadership must aid in the development of a series of strategic steps that push the church to become healthy. This must be done at a pace that is doable for the church, and it requires wisdom and insight that can only be gleaned by pastors and church leadership who have the competencies for this task. This chapter will set the stage for the journey ahead, setting forth initial steps on how pastors and church leadership can ready themselves for this journey. By taking this deliberative journey to survey the terrain of church revitalization before fully embarking on the journey, pastors and church leadership can avoid missteps and achieve greater resiliency in the revitalization process.

BIBLICAL AND THEOLOGICAL FOUNDATIONS FOR CHURCH REVITALIZATION

What New Testament concepts relate to the process of church revitalization? While the New Testament gives us valuable information regarding the life of the early church, the early church dealt more with efforts to plant churches than to revitalize them. Paul's establishment of new churches is different from church revitalization. Some parts of the New Testament, however, do relate to church revitalization. In his third missionary journey, Paul returns to existing churches to strengthen and develop them (Acts 19–21). But in a general sense, Paul wrestles in his letters with issues of doctrinal purity, church unity, internal disorder, and moral issues. The churches he wrote to were young and in need of basic instruction, not revitalization. The Pastoral Epistles (1–2 Timothy, Titus), Paul's latest letters, show greater church development. He describes elder and deacon ministry at length (1 Tim. 3:1–13), and gives evidence that ministry to widows has already been developed (1 Tim. 5:3–16). However, even these ministries would be implemented in a contemporary church plant from the beginning. It is certainly possible in church revitalization that foundational realities about church life might be missed from its inception and that the initial instruction Paul gave to these early churches would need to be established late in the development of a contemporary church.[2] Even so, directly relating the early churches in Acts and Paul's letters to church revitalization fails to recognize that church revitalization typically occurs in churches older than those described in the New Testament.

The closest parallel to church revitalization in the New Testament is found in the opening chapters of the book of Revelation (Rev. 2–3). Since the dating of the book of Revelation is around AD 95–96,[3] the churches described there have already experienced birth, growth, and decline. These letters that Jesus sends to the churches reveal a complex evaluation of each church situation. Without intervention a church could cease to exist (Rev. 2:5). Yet each church is called to see its strengths and repent of its weaknesses. This concept of leaning into strengths and ridding the church of critical weaknesses is more akin to the process of church revitalization. The call to the church in the book of Revelation is not a complete restart, but a serious adjustment so that obedience to Christ and revitalization can be attained.

DEFINING CHURCH REVITALIZATION ON A SPECTRUM

One of the difficulties of church revitalization is defining what it is. Many conversations concerning church revitalization stall at the place of definition. While it is warranted to spend time and energy on giving a precise definition of what church revitalization looks like in a particular situation, it seems clear that a one-size-fits-all definition will either be too broad to be helpful or too narrow and omit certain efforts in revitalization. Rather than defining church revitalization with a precise definition, it seems better to approach defining church revitalization along a spectrum or levels of need. Four terms can be helpful in understanding the level of revitalization necessary

---

2 Douglas Moo, *A Theology of Paul and His Letters: The Gift of the New Realm in Christ*, Biblical Theology of the New Testament (Grand Rapids: Zondervan, 2021), 43–52.

3 Robert Thomas, *Revelation 1–7: An Exegetical Commentary* (Chicago: Moody, 1992), 20–22. Thomas makes a compelling case for a late date of the book of Revelation.

in a particular church situation. The four terms are *refresh, renovate, restore,* and *replant.*[4]

Refresh Revitalization			
Duration of Decline	**Church Resources**	**Spiritual Vitality**	**Average Time for Revitalization**
Fewer than five years	Capable church membership, maintained facilities, stable finances	Spiritual metrics (conversions, discipleship, etc.) relatively healthy.	Two to four years

Refresh Revitalization

The "refresh" level in church revitalization requires the least invasive interventions to bring the church back to spiritual health. Typically, in a refresh revitalization church decline has not been long term (fewer than five years). The church has resources that enable it to quickly turn around, such as strong membership, an adequate facility, and reasonable financial footing. Further, while there has been decline in conversions, worship attendance, small groups, and ministry participation, there is still a strong nucleus of support. A refresh is typically necessary after a difficult season in the life of the church. In a refresh situation, a previous pastoral staff member may have struggled, and the church entered into a season of decline. The decline was not greatly disruptive, but nevertheless the church is less healthy than in previous seasons. A fresh vision within the church could enable it to lean into untapped resources to bring about revitalization. A refresh revitalization could see clear results within two to three years.

---

4   I am indebted to John Ewart, professor of missions and pastoral leadership and associate vice president for global theological initiatives and ministry centers at Southeastern Baptist Theological Seminary, for developing this concept.

Renovate Revitalization			
Duration of Decline	Church Resources	Spiritual Vitality	Average Time for Revitalization
Five to fifteen years	Reduced church membership, deferred maintenance on facilities, strained finances	Spiritual metrics (conversions, discipleship, etc.) in decline	Five to seven years

Renovate Revitalization

The "renovate" level in church revitalization requires more serious interventions to bring the church back to spiritual health. Typically, in a renovate revitalization the church decline has been long term (between five and fifteen years). The church's resources were expended to a great amount during this time. The membership is weakened, the facility has deferred maintenance, and the financial situation is strained. Further, there has been decline in conversions, worship attendance, small groups, and ministry participation, and this decline has seriously weakened the spiritual ministry of the church. A renovation typically comes after several pastoral transitions. The church has steadily declined even after various attempts at seeing new life established. The church has lost a sense of mission and is generally disheartened at the state of affairs. A renovation will require structural changes in the church, along with fresh vision and capable leadership. To see results in a renovate revitalization, churches should not expect to see clear results until year five.

Restore Revitalization			
Duration of Decline	Church Resources	Spiritual Vitality	Average Time for Revitalization
More than fifteen years	Small church membership, building in disrepair, inadequate finances	Mission jettisoned to merely survive	Five to eight years

Restore Revitalization

The "restore" level in church revitalization requires dramatic interventions to bring the church back to spiritual health. Typically, in a restore revitalization the church decline has been long term, likely for generations (more than fifteen years). The church has a very inward, often small membership; the facility is typically greatly neglected; and the financial situation is focused on survival, not mission. Strangely, in some restoration situations the church has a reasonable amount of money in the bank, but this is viewed as a security for the payment of future bills and property maintenance, not strategic mission initiatives. The concept of conversions, discipleship through groups, increasing worship attendance, and ministry participation are often outside the purview of metrics the church understands. Many members who are in a church that needs restoration hope only that the church will exist throughout their lifetime. Some see no future for the church other than a nice place for their funeral to be conducted and hope to see the church remain long enough for this to happen. While this is a sad state of affairs, it is not all that uncommon for churches to face this reality. While churches in this state are not without hope, the generational patterns of unhealthy behavior will require dramatic interventions to bring the church back to life. Dramatic interventions will be resisted by a congregation that is focused on mere survival, not thriving mission. Church leadership, ideally starting with a lead pastor, will need to win the trust of the congregation and be willing to work for the long term—between five to eight years—to see real revitalization.

Replant Revitalization			
Duration of Decline	**Church Resources**	**Spiritual Vitality**	**Average Time for Revitalization**
More than fifteen years	A building with deferred maintenance and an aging church membership	Imminent death threatened due to lack of attendees	More quickly (one to three years) because a new leadership team with a new core group starts a fresh work

Replant Revitalization

The "replant" level in church revitalization, which is barely within the domain of church revitalization, is basically a church coming to terms with the reality that it does not have the strength to continue without outside intervention. A replant is more closely related to church planting than to revitalization. In revitalization, some aspects of the previous church exist in the new emerging entity. In many replants, the old identity is lost, a new identity is established, and the old church property may be repurposed for a new mission work. This is certainly superior to the closing and selling of the church property. However, replanting is basically a new work using the resources of an older church to accomplish a new vision with a new congregation. Some of the members may become a part of this new work, but the work will be fundamentally different from the previous work.

The Difference Between Revitalization and Replant[5]

Revitalization: The supernatural work of God that restores health and vitality in a plateaued or declining church, evidenced by submission to God's Word, right relationships among members, and a renewed commitment to Great Commission ministry.
Revitalization: *existing church + existing leaders + existing structure + history + renewed/new effort.*

Replanting: The process in which members of a church facing imminent closure discern God's leadership to dissolve their current ministry and work with other churches or denominational bodies to begin a new church for a new season of ministry in their community.
Replant: *new qualified/skilled leader + existing people + new structures/ approaches + outside partners + new people + history*

---

5   These are the "officially" adopted definitions of the Replant Team at North American Mission Board for replanting and revitalization.

A SPIRITUAL JOURNEY

At times church revitalization may require other church leaders to step in and initiate change, but for practical purposes this book will address the typical situation where pastoral staff are the primary change agents in leading church-revitalization initiatives. So where do we begin on this journey toward church revitalization? It is important to know that this journey will be a prayerful and spiritual journey. It may feel intuitive to start the process scheming about your church; however, the ideal place to start the revitalization journey is with a pastor's relationship with God. Pastors and church leadership are a major conduit for church revitalization. The spiritual resources a pastor has will enable him to negotiate not only the failures in church revitalization but also the successes.

It may feel cliché to solidify and celebrate your conversion as a pastor, but it is not. A pastor must know that he has turned from his sin and self and put his faith in Jesus Christ. A pastor must be confident in the power of the gospel to change his own life before he will have that passion to share the gospel with others.[6] Also, a pastor must then know the daily joy of walking in God's presence. It will be from the overflow of a healthy Christian life that church revitalization can be undertaken. Even if success can be accomplished by a pastor whose spiritual life is not in order, the pressure of achieving church revitalization can at best lead to burnout and at worst to moral compromise. Pastors' and other church leaders' spiritual readiness must be assessed.[7] A means to analyze a pastor's spiritual readiness for the task ahead is to examine his past behavior. If a sin issue has emerged in the past, the behavior will likely emerge in the future under the stress of church revitalization. Therefore, personal spiritual preparedness is

---

6   Scot McKnight, *The King Jesus Gospel: The Original Good News Revisited* (Grand Rapids: Zondervan, 2016). McKnight argues the need to clarify the concept of gospel especially as it related to conversion.

7   Dallas Willard, *The Spirit of the Disciplines* (San Francisco: HarperSanFrancisco, 1988); and Richard Foster, *Celebration of Discipline* (San Francisco, Harper & Row, 1978) are great resources for setting forth a plan for spiritual disciplines.

essential for any pastor or church leader undertaking such a spiritually strenuous task.

The path to preparedness may not be through greater striving but through a greater understanding of grace. It is easy to become performance-driven and not rest in grace. At the heart of the doctrine of conversion is the concept of grace. Grace is receiving what you do not deserve. The Christian's standing before God is not based on works. It is based on sheer grace.[8] Most pastors do not need to be taught this theologically. They have it worked out intellectually. Pastors, however, so often enter the pastorate with a work-based, performance-based attitude. A pastor becomes too personally connected with the success and failure of the church, and his identity becomes wrapped up in being a pastor and not merely being a Christian who has been lavished with grace. It is important when entering church revitalization that a pastor's personal identity does not depend on church success.[9] If pastors and church leaders find that church success is critical to their sense of identity, then it will be important to seek out a spiritual mentor to communicate God's grace to them so that they can rest in grace and not in personal accomplishment. For example, it will be commonplace for a congregation to refer to pastoral staff as "pastor." A congregation may even have a hard time separating the office of pastor from the person. It is wonderful that God has led pastors into ministry. It is a noble vocation. However, pastors need to remember that they have an identity outside of being a pastor. There are other vocations that pastors hold such as spouse, parent, and friend. Pastors should be wary of fusing their identity with the functions of pastoral ministry and the success and failure of a particular church situation. A pastor must learn to rest on God's unconditional love and grace.

---

8   Philip Yancey, *What's So Amazing about Grace?* (Grand Rapids: Zondervan, 2002), and Brennan Manning, *The Ragamuffin Gospel: Good News for the Bedraggled, Beat-Up, and Burnt Out* (Colorado Springs: Multnomah, 2005). These books explore the power of grace to bring about wholeness in the life of a person.

9   R. Kent Hughes and Barbara Hughes, *Liberating Ministry from the Success Syndrome* (Wheaton, IL: Crossway, 2008), 35–44.

Jesus is sufficient to change the lives of the people in our churches; Jesus merely *uses* pastors and church leaders to aid in this process.

Pastors' and church leaders' primary goal should be to see people come to faith in Christ and develop in Christlikeness. This singular focus should inform all church strategies and initiatives. Further, if a pastor does not have a stable spiritual life, the goal of people-pleasing and crowd-building can eclipse disciple-making. Church revitalization can be undertaken with wrong motivations, which can be subtle and deceptive. It is necessary that a pastor's desire for church revitalization be truly for the good of others and not a subtle means to fortify personal identity. The revitalization journey must be taken for the good of those within the church and the community. A pastor must engage in his own process of spiritual formation so that he can be an appropriate conduit of grace and spiritual health to those around him. The ministry is a unique calling: a pastor is the tool that will be used to lead a church. A pastor who has his own heart in order will enhance his spiritual effectiveness in discipling others.[10]

A SPECIFIC CALLING

Church revitalization requires a pastor, among the other church leaders, to recognize a specific calling to revitalize a specific church. Starting with paid pastoral staff, he must take time to carefully evaluate his calling to church revitalization as a specific ministry assignment. Church revitalization is only one method in God's multifaceted kingdom work. There are many places where God can work such as church planting, international missions, and mercy ministries. Church planting is a noble calling. There are many places in the United States where there is a need for a new church presence. Further, the lostness of the world is a strong reason to contemplate the international mission field. There are many places in the world where there is no need for church revitalization because there has never been a church. In an ever-changing world, ministry oppor-

---

10   Peter Scazzero, *Emotionally Healthy Spirituality* (San Francisco: HarperOne, 2017), 39–70.

tunities are endless. There are new platforms on which a person can minister. It is important to evaluate the various options before settling on church revitalization. Even if you decided to fully commit to church revitalization, the revitalized church still has a role to play in aiding in church planting, missions involvement, and various mercy ministries. Church revitalization is merely choosing the location from which a pastor and other church leaders can participate in God's multifaceted kingdom work.

A serious evaluation needs to be made as to why a pastor believes God has called him to church revitalization. It is important to write these reasons down. A pastor or church leader may need to consult this list, especially on the bad days. Some of the positive reasons for engaging in church revitalization are seeing new life come to an established church, building on a church's legacy, seeing a gospel presence reemerge in a community, and participating in God's redemption plan in the context of the local church.[11] There is a unique wonder in seeing a church resurrected in a community where life was previously limited. A clear theological reason to do ministry from the location of the local church is the unique love that God has for the church. While many other places of ministry are noble, the context of ministry from inside a local church receives God's most intense love.

Pastors along with other church leaders will need to develop deep convictions that church revitalization is in fact God's place for them in this season of their life. The process of church revitalization will require a great deal of work. For example, there are challenging seasons in the life of a pastor. A young pastor who is newly married may not be able to take on this task. A pastor who has many family obligations either due to children or other family situations may need to think through the sacrifices. An older pastor who may be seeking to serve in a chaplain role, not as a change agent, may not be the right fit for

---

11 Mark Clifton, *Reclaiming the Glory: Revitalizing Dying Churches* (Nashville: B&H, 2016). The thesis of this book is that revitalization should be pursued to reclaim the glory of God by making the church a visible witness of the power of God in a community.

this endeavor. For church revitalization to work, the right season in the life of the church and the life of a pastor must merge.

BECOMING A VISIONARY

Once a pastor can discern that he is spiritually ready for this task, it is time to start thinking and dreaming about the church. It is important to see the future, what things can be, what the church can be, and to see this vision clearly. To lead in a church revitalization, a pastor must see what the church does not see, at least at first. A pastor must be able to envision what a revived presence in the community would look like. A pastor must be able to see beyond the immediate situation to a future situation when many of the obstacles and problems would be resolved. This will require a great deal of vision and mental toughness. A pastor must believe this vision because there will be many situations that will make him question its feasibility.[12] For example, a pastor should not be surprised when the congregation would prefer him to attempt ministry objectives without their enthusiastic participation. In some church revitalizations, there are long seasons of dryness. Congregants want to believe in better days for the church, but past experiences have been so painful that they struggle to see a bright future.

A pastor must become optimistic about a church situation that many have grown pessimistic about. A pastor must be able to negotiate the difficult tension between what things can be and how things are. The congregants will often just see what is. They will have lower expectations than pastors and maybe other church leaders. Pastors and church leaders will need to accept that these expectations have been set over a long period of time. The reason the church needs revitalization is that the execution of ministry objectives has not been met. Sadly, many churches are reluctantly satisfied with survival. In some contexts, mere survival has not been easy. Some churches have endured member conflicts, pastoral conflict, community demographic

---

12   Andy Stanley, *Visioneering: God's Blueprint for Developing and Maintaining Vision* (Colorado Springs: Multnomah, 1999), 17–28.

shifts, and even denominational disruption. A pastor needs to be able to see the hard work it has taken for the church to exist even in the form that the church is currently in. Typically, many members within the church have personally sacrificed for the church to be in whatever form it currently stands.

The church revitalizer needs to develop a compelling vision of what the church can be while not losing sight of the beauty and sacrifice that is already there. This balance will bring a great deal of sanity to the situation. It is an all-too-common mistake to not see the beauty in the church that is there. If the vision is so future-oriented that the people get the sense that what they have worked to build is insufficient, then one's role as a pastor will be greatly harmed. So, a balanced assessment of what it has taken for the church to exist in this form, along with the brighter future that the church can have, must be held in tension.

DEVELOPING THE NEEDED COMPETENCIES

Church revitalization requires a pastor to develop competencies that will guide him through this process. The following questions will help a pastor assess his own level of conviction in certain areas. A church revitalizer must not only have tactical skills in organizing but also possess the emotional intelligence to lead an established church. Here are seven questions to ponder as a pastor or other church leader thinks about this journey.

Can You Present Solutions Without Being Perceived as the Problem?

The reality of problems and solutions becomes complex in a church. There is no clear agreement on the problems and the solutions. Especially in conflict-riddled churches, the main goal of some church members is merely keeping the peace or status quo. Admitting a problem and seeking solutions requires changes and change often creates conflict. Often there are hidden stakeholders that desire for the church to exist in a certain way. When a solution is presented that will in some way affect these often-hidden stakeholders, a pastor or even another church leader can be labeled as a problem.

To an inexperienced pastor, being labeled a problem when presenting prayed-through solutions can strike at the gut level. Most
pastors have pursued the ministry out of a desire to see a change in
people, have a great love for those people, and are natural helpers.
Pastors enjoy being an agent of comfort to those who are struggling.
So, it is jarring for some pastors when in this loving spirit they
set forth a solution to help the church and are labeled unhelpful
and a "problem creator." Moving a church toward a brighter future will often require being in dissonance with the congregation.
This dissonance does not mean that a pastor is a problem or even
that what he is doing is wrong. This is a healthy part of church
revitalization. The issue arises when a pastor takes these criticisms
personally, begins to think less of the congregation, and loses his
love for certain people within the church. This unfortunate change
of perspective can lead a pastor down poor paths and toward actually
becoming part of the problem. A pastor will need to develop the
conviction that even if his solutions are not seen as such, he will
not take it personally and will see it rather as one step in a larger
process of change.

Can You Change Existing Structures Internally?
A church has structures that exist before a pastor arrives. A pastor will
have to work within the current system as his starting point. While
there is often opportunity to change the way a church operates, the
change in operations must be accomplished within the structures
that presently exist. A pastor will need to discern which structures
can remain unchanged, which structures can be enhanced, and which
structures may need to be removed. The pastor must accept the
structures that are there and learn to live within them for a season.
It is wise for a pastor to live within a system for six months to a year
upon arrival at a new church, learning what the structures are and
how they operate. Churches are often very fluid even when they have
written protocols. Therefore, it is unwise for a pastor to think that he
will be able to understand how a church operates by merely reading
the bylaws or reviewing a church manual.

Church structures are formed out of experiences, powerful personalities, and many other complex factors. The structure may not seem intuitive and may hinder the church from achieving its goals. There is a rationale for why things are the way they are. Any attempt to quickly change the structures will likely only temporarily shift them. Church structures are naturally prone to drift back to the place they are in presently. Therefore, a pastor must develop a deep conviction to understand how the church operates, so that real structural change can occur.[13] It is easy to change names and titles without a true change in function. If the pastor wants deep change in a church, this will require learning and strategic movement.

Can You Embrace a Church History, Not Create One?

Church revitalization requires entering a church that has a history. Any church that exists for any period has a history. Many churches that need church revitalization have a long history. There are few things more important than learning the history of a church. The actions and behavioral patterns of a church give you much information about it.

Unless a church has had a very bad event in its past, it is often very fond of its history. For families within the church that have a long-term relationship in a particular geographical region, the church is a monument of many past lives. The embracing of a church's history is an important part of becoming a true pastor to the people of the church. Whether a pastor is fully aware of it or not, he is becoming a part of this history.

It is appropriate for a pastor to see his work as part of a continuation of a larger work that has been happening since the church was born. One of the beauties of church revitalization is a pastor's desire to contribute a bright chapter into a long history of a church. The pastor must learn the story of the church, tell the story of the church, and thoughtfully contribute to its history. The pastor also needs to tell himself the story of the church and then rehearse the chapter of church

---

13 Steve Smith, *The Increasing Church Capacity Guidebook: Designing and Linking the 18 Systems* (Lakeland, FL: Church Equippers, 2015), 5–20.

history he envisions during his pastorate. One day the pastor will leave the church. It is important for him to contemplate on the front end what his legacy at this church, and for God's kingdom, will be.

Can You Be Patient and Strategic?

Strategic patience is a critical conviction. Change in church life often goes much more slowly than a pastor desires. Further, pushing too hard in a situation will set the overall strategy back. For real change, timing is everything. In church life ideas must be presented informally, formally, and repeatedly before there is sufficient congregational buy-in. A pastor will have to engage in a push-and-pull with the congregation that desires to move toward revitalization.

Strategic patience will start as a conviction and develop into a skill over time. There will be an intuitive sense of when to push and when to stop pushing for an idea. Learning the personalities and structures of the church will enable a pastor to know when enough is enough. There is no advantage to aggressively pushing through decisions in church life. When this happens, the result is only that it will take more time to effect the next change. Strategic patience usually requires a pastor to start slowly and build momentum over time. Often in successful church revitalizations, small changes lead to bigger changes as success happens and trust is earned. A pastor must take the long view and be ready to stay at a church for a minimum of five years.[14]

Can You Engage in Negotiation and Accept Compromise?

Negotiation and compromise will always be part of leadership. In church revitalization, the conviction to compromise is very important. In other environments, there are clearer lines of authority and decision-making. A pastor is both a leader and an employee. Therefore, the congregation will be willing to hear a pastor's vision for the church, but they may also have ideas that are valid. Being able to negotiate and keep people

---

14   Jack L. Daniel, *Patient Catalyst: Leading Church Revitalization* (South Easton, MA: Overseed, 2018). Daniel sees timing and patience as key leadership characteristics that bring about revitalization.

on the team is an important aspect of leadership. If a pastor becomes overly committed to a vision for the church and becomes inflexible, then the relationship with the church will likely not end well.

It is important at the beginning of the revitalization process to embrace the reality that many goals a pastor will develop for the church will not come to fruition in the manner he desires. The positive is that sometimes the process of negotiation and compromise will produce better overall results for the church. There is often wisdom in having broad consultation, even when the resulting compromise does not accomplish what is ultimately best. There will likely be several of these situations in a revitalization. A pastor will have to learn to live with this. It is not wise to perpetually readdress areas where compromise was hard fought to achieve. Pastors in church-revitalization situations have to learn how to listen, give concrete ideas, negotiate with conflicting ideas, and bring the church to a reasonable middle position. This will be a constant in church life. This is not just difficult to develop the skill; the emotional toll of having to listen and address opinions that seem to lack rationality can lead to discouragement and anger. Therefore, the pastor must make a strong conviction to give himself to this process.

Can You Embrace Progress, Not Perfection?

The goal of a pastor is to move the church in a spiritually healthy direction. A pastor must be content with progress toward health. Perfection is not needed. A church that has existed for a long time has taken detours on the road to vitality. These detours will likely continue even during this new season because this is the nature of church communities, where a group of diverse people attempts to achieve collective goals. It will be important to constantly assess the positive things that are happening, and to document even small steps toward health. There is often a sense among pastors that although many good things have happened in their church, there are still many more things that need to happen.

A pastor of an established church must reckon with the fact that not every problem will be solved during his pastorate. There will be challenges and problems that will be left for future generations to address. Only a limited number of things can be changed in a given period. God is gracious to give a pastor several ministry objectives that he can complete to move the church toward health even without seeing the church achieve the optimum health. A pastor needs to be emotionally settled with that. God may allow a pastor to see great spiritual health occur. If so, there is great cause to rejoice. Often in many church situations, however, progress is made but optimum spiritual health is not achieved. This is not settling for second-best. The current progress toward health is likely all the church is willing or able to accomplish at this time in its life. As a church revitalizer, you must accept progress toward health, not perfection.

Can You Pastor the Church You Would Like to Create?

Pastors engaging in revitalization have a vision for what they would like the church to become. Often, they long for a larger staff, a robust music program, a dynamic children's ministry, an innovative student ministry, small groups, community ministry, and so forth. The pastor himself must be able to rise to the challenge of leading this dynamic church. Changes toward these realities may therefore need to be slow and incremental. Some churches can outgrow the leaders that brought them through a revitalization. Church revitalization demands not only that the church body grow but that a pastor and church leadership grow as well. Many pastors who have hoped that a larger staff would solve their problems come to realize staff oversight and management are one of their largest problems. A revitalizer needs to be careful what he hopes for. Further, with a growing and thriving congregation, a pastor will be pushed to grow, change styles of leadership, relate differently to the congregation, and continually adjust his role in the church. This is good and healthy but is often an unforeseen reality in church revitalizations. A pastor must also come to grips with the reality that some leaders will be great in one season in the life of the church but will not thrive in another season. A church can be moving toward health, but leaders who cannot make the transition will sadly be left behind. This can be grievous to a pastor who has helped the church become healthier only to watch as some who were with him early on do not have the skill set to continue in the same leadership level as in the past.[15]

Becoming a Church Revitalizer

The goal of this book is to enable a pastor or church leader to start the process of becoming a church revitalizer. It will not be sufficient to merely learn skills and tips. There will be important tasks to accomplish; however, these skills and tips are insufficient to prepare a leader emotionally and spiritually for what lies ahead. Revitalizers can take a realistic but optimistic view of churches. They can see things within a church that are doable based on the spiritual health of the people and attempt to accomplish them. They love the church and its intrinsic beauty. Revitalizers enjoy the simple worship and fellowship among Christians. They desire better for the church but can deeply love the church that is there. They will genuinely exude a pastoral quality, encouraging people to follow them, because of their own disposition and spiritual qualities.

This book alone cannot make someone this type of person. However, it can be a guide to this path that other pastors have traveled. Pastors should be encouraged on this journey. The church needs good shepherds. There is a spiritual hunger among so many in the culture, people who are looking for spiritual wholeness. Pastors have an opportunity to learn how to minister in this unique time, to a unique group of people, and to see God do a unique work through the church. It is worth the training and sacrifice to experience the joy of what lies ahead.

---

15 John Maxwell, *5 Levels of Leadership: Proven Steps to Maximize Your Potential* (New York: CenterStreet, 2011), and Gary L. McIntosh, *Taking Your Church to the Next Level: What Got You Here Won't Get You There* (Grand Rapids: Baker Books, 2009). Both of these books argue the need for leaders to grow and change as the leaders' situation and church situation develops.

CLARIFYING A CHURCH'S CONVICTIONS

How do revitalizers answer the question, "What is a church?" This question gets varied answers from pastors and church members alike. For many people focusing on the practicalities of church revitalization, classes in ecclesiology (the doctrine of the church) seem distant and potentially irrelevant to the needs at hand. This chapter argues that how a church leader answers the question "What is a church?" will radically affect what type of church emerges from the revitalization process. This chapter attempts to uncover how core convictions about the nature of the church will define what type of church revitalization will happen.

Within Protestantism, many decry that lack of unity within the church. There seems to be a different type of church for every theological whim and personal preference. While the unity of the church is an issue that requires serious contemplation and dialogue, the truth is that every church leader creates a church based on some theological foundation, and this foundation defines what type of church it will become. It is commonplace for church leaders who are attempting to begin the process of revitalization to think their church will be a place for everyone. This is a noble ambition and an aspirational goal, but it will not work. The church should attempt to be as welcoming to all groups as possible. However, decisions must be made about many areas of church life, and these decisions will necessarily delimit the type of church that will emerge and often influence the type of person the church will reach.

THE ESSENCE OF A CHURCH

Church leaders must have some core convictions about the nature of the church. Ideally, these convictions are born out of biblical study with an awareness of church history. Without serious engagement on these topics, only later in the revitalization process will church leaders discover what type of church has been made. There have been several issues that the church has struggled with throughout church history: the issue of linkage to the apostles, the need for purity and holiness, and the mandate of mission, to mention a few. Protestants historically have defined the church through marks. A mark is a specific function of the church, such as preaching the gospel, which is a necessary requirement for a church to be classified as a true church.[1] A common mantra is that the church is not a building but a body of people. While this is true in one sense, the church is much more than a mere gathering of people. Further, beyond the historical-doctrinal discussion of the nature of the church are the practical realities. There are many different church styles. These include organic house churches, recovery churches, multisite churches, seeker churches, ancient-future churches, city-reaching churches, and attractional churches.[2] The interplay between the historic discussions of the nature of the church and the practical realities of missional appropriateness in a cultural context will require thoughtful analysis.

1   Alister E. McGrath, ed., *Theology: The Basic Readings*, 3rd ed. (Oxford: Wiley Blackwell, 2018), 162–66.
2   Elmer Towns, Ed Stetzer, and Warren Bird, *11 Innovations in the Local Church: How Today's Leaders Can Learn, Discern and Move into the Future* (Ventura, CA: Regal, 2007). This book gives a good overview of many varieties of churches.

The church comes together with some degree of organization for the purpose of accomplishing certain functions. Frustrated church leaders who realize that the church is more than a mere gathering of people struggle when their congregation meets together for less-than-ideal aims. Church leadership must therefore clarify the aims it is pursuing before becoming too exasperated. The main historical marks of a church for Protestants have included preaching the gospel, the ordinances of the church, and church discipline.[3] Few church leaders today, however, hold these marks as distinguishing, especially church discipline. Before a revitalization is going to occur, it would be wise for the church leaders to know what they believe the marks of a church to be. They can then clearly emphasize these marks to the gathered church.[4]

LOCATING THE CHURCH'S TRADITION

There is currently a rise in the nondenominational spirit. On the one hand, this is reasonable. Many faithful churchgoers have experienced bitter church fights. These leave an indelible mark on the souls of those who endure these experiences. Therefore, an open hand of generosity and a gracious spirit to avoid such bitter disputes is warranted. A general sense of charity is important when charting out one's understanding of Christian conviction and the nature of the church. This charitable spirit, however, will not stop the reality of making lines of demarcation. In a sinful world where people are unable to interpret the Scriptures perfectly and understand the things of God with profound clarity, some version of denominational affiliation is inevitable.

To believe that one can merely be a community church that has convictions wide enough for all is naive. Landing in a denominational tradition does not mean that one must close off all other traditions. Leaders can charitably and firmly locate their church within a tradition and then appreciate the goodness of other traditions. It seems best

---

3   Timothy George, *Theology of the Reformers* (Nashville: B&H Academic, 2013).

4   Mark Dever, *9 Marks of a Heathy Church*, 3rd ed. (Wheaton, IL: Crossway, 2013). Mark Dever is to be commended for recovering the Protestant idea of the marks of the church and encouraging pastors to think through the distinguishing aspects of church life.

to commit to a denomination and work to make that denomination the best version it can be rather than placing oneself on a theological and ecclesiological island outside all denominations. One way a person locates their church in a denomination or Christian tradition is through the affirmation of a doctrinal statement. When doctrine is solidified, it makes clear boundary markers. There are many great doctrinal statements. Church leaders and church members should carefully read these doctrinal statements and decide what to affirm and what to deny. Affirming on the front end what a church believes gives it the ability to know what it will likely become. Without this clarity of conviction on the front end, what is developed will likely be an accident of history. Sometimes, church leaders realize that the denominational affiliation that aided the church in the past is no longer sufficient for the convictions of the present moment. Other times, a revitalization occurs within a denominational structure that no longer represents the beliefs of the gathered congregation. These are difficult situations, but they can be avoided by thoughtfulness on the front end and by a clear doctrinal statement. The doctrinal turbulence that has occurred in virtually every mainline denomination should caution church revitalizers to ensure that the denomination affirms the core convictions of the church leaders and congregation at large.[5]

HOW DO WE ORGANIZE?

The intricacies of theology become very practical in the church when the church begins to organize in any form. It is a nice thought that the simplicity of an unstructured house-church model can exist as a church develops, but this is not how human organization or church life works. There are offices in a church. The two main offices of a church are the office of pastor and deacon. The church must decide how these categories of leadership will be expressed within the church. It seems misguided to not have at minimum these two offices defined and active in some capacity. Church life, however, is messier than the simplicity of

---

5   Mark Noll, *The Old Religion in a New World: The History of North American Christianity* (Grand Rapids: Eerdmans, 2002).

these two offices might imply. Most churches also have ministry teams, committees, and other forms of organization, not to mention paid staff that do not fall into the category of pastor or deacon. The church at large should likewise be involved in ministry. Without a clear-eyed plan for the role of pastor and deacon in the larger context of ministry teams, committees, staff, and church membership, there will be deep confusion about how the church is organized. There are many different expressions of church leadership that do not seem to show awareness of the biblical perimeters. A simple flowchart of organization will be necessary for theological clarity and practical application of leadership within the church. If there is clarity for those in a leadership role in the church, then there will also be some level of requirements for the position. The Bible states requirements for pastors and deacons (1 Tim. 3:1–13). For positions outside these biblically prescribed positions, there must be basic levels of requirements as well.

Elders and Pastoral Staff

Plural elder leadership is a commonly embraced model for the pastoral office. Even within this model there are many varieties. A team-based approach to leadership can still come in many forms. Plural elder leadership could denote a leader among equals, who functions like a solo senior pastor with greater accountability. The vision and direction still primarily come from one person, but the vision is vetted through counsel. Other models that embrace a plural elder leadership role have a team of pastors that function at the same level of authority and share the leadership and teaching of the church. Some team models concentrate most of the decision-making authority to the elders, whereas in other models the elders merely lead the church with robust input from the congregation. To merely state that one embraces a team-based elder model leaves many questions unanswered.[6]

---

6   Chad Brand and Stan Norman, eds., *Perspectives on Church Government: Five Views* (Nashville: B&H, 2004); Paul Engle and Steven Cowan, eds., *Who Runs the Church? Four Views on Church Government* (Grand Rapids: Zondervan, 2004).

Those churches that do not embrace an elder approach to leadership can default to a staff-led approach to leadership. A staff-led model organizes the leadership of the church around the various ministry functions of the church and the leadership of these areas. This approach often has its own hierarchy in which the senior pastor has the ultimate responsibility to manage and organize the staff. Even if a church does not embrace this model fully, if a church has staff that does not fit into the offices of elder or deacon then some type of organization and management of these staff is important. Further, staff that are full-time or part-time at a church provide more time and attention to these ministries by nature of their paid status. Someone must be responsible for training, enrichment, evaluation, and unfortunately termination of these positions. In church life, the management of larger staffs can be a great joy and burden. In more complex church structures, there are pastors, deacons, ministry teams, paid staff, and members. These must be organized and managed appropriately toward appropriate ends. Many pastors who are leading church revitalization long for a larger staff where all the responsibility does not fall back on them. However, this may or may not be the case; the larger the staff, the more complex the personnel issues become. In this new world of hiring and firing, a church that has a moderately sized staff will need separate guidance from those with knowledge in human resources and personnel management merely to operate appropriately in accordance with the rights of employees and laws of employment.[7]

The Role of Deacons

Deacons should have an ample role to play in church structure. Biblical deaconship (2 Tim. 3:8–12) can easily be lost in the flurry of administrative activities in a church. Deacons have as their primarily role the care of those who are most easily forgotten and overlooked. In the necessity of administration, the church must protect the deacon ministry from becoming overly involved in church administration to

---

7   Joan Pynes, *Human Resources Management for Public and Nonprofit Organizations*, 4th ed. (San Francisco: Jossey-Bass, 2013).

the neglect of the biblically prescribed ministry to the widow, poor, and needy. When a church structure is functioning poorly, the deacons tend to become entangled in matters of administration that are not directly related to being a minister of mercy. A properly functioning deacon ministry should unleash practical ministry within a church, and the otherwise overlooked should be looked after with great care.[8]

Meaningful Church Membership

This issue of church commitment raises the issue of church membership. Some churches either do not keep track of church membership or church membership has become so diluted that it is virtually without merit. It seems biblically wise and practically important to have some clear understanding of the expectation not only for leaders but also for members. This should not be done in a harsh way, but the simple reality is that being part of any organization requires some understanding of and obligation to the participant. In a church revitalization, a pastor will likely inherit a group of church members who have various views of what membership means. It will be important to come to some conclusion slowly but deliberately on what it means to be part of their local church. The church will struggle to raise up quality leadership within the congregation if it does not have clear requirements of what committed church membership means.[9]

The Process of Decision-Making

Once we gather and organize, we agree and unfortunately disagree. In the area of disagreement especially, a clear-eyed plan on who can make what decision is very important. Without a clear plan for how decisions are made, the church will devolve into the loudest or most

---

8   Alexander Strauch, *The New Testament Deacon: The Church's Minister of Mercy* (Colorado Springs: Lewis & Roth, 1992).

9   John Hammett, *Biblical Foundations for Baptist Churches*, 2nd ed. (Grand Rapids: Kregel, 2019), 91–144. I am indebted to John Hammett, who reawakened the need for meaningful, regenerate church membership. Thom Rainer, in *I Am a Church Member* (Nashville, B&H, 2013), gives practical steps on how to function as an engaged church member.

influential person being able to sway the church in their own direction. There are several models for who is the ultimate earthly authority. It is nice to say that Jesus is the head of the church and that the church should follow him. This is true theologically, but practically the church is looking for actual ways decisions are made. In a world of sin, any sole group firmly retaining decision-making usually creates problems. However, the opposite problem occurs when the church does not know who is in charge. The debate over church models is still part of the ongoing conversation. The trend seems to be moving in a direction of team models versus solo leader models. This change is likely influenced by the abuses of pastors without proper account-ability in the areas of finances and morality. It does not seem wise for one person to hold decision-making authority without accountability.

Developing an Organization Structure

The way leadership works is that there are few leaders and many fol-lowers. If there are many leaders and few followers, then leadership is not actually happening. The question that must be addressed is, "Do church members have a voice in decision-making?" If they do have a voice, then how is their voice heard? In more top-down models of church governance, a bishop might make decisions for the congrega-tion. If the congregational majority does not affirm these decisions, they have very little recourse. In more congregationally governed models, the congregation has a way to make its voice heard and hold the leaders over them to account as needed. A congregational form of government can be detrimental as well. If the congregation is re-quired to provide input on most decisions, then decision-making can often be slow and contentious. Majority rule in churches seems to be a fair way of operating for many, because this is how many social decisions are made. In a church where decisions must be arrived at by majority and not consensus, unhealthy posturing and fracturing can occur. While a majority may be necessary to make decisions in certain social matters, it seems more appropriate for the church to hold an ideal higher than a majority overruling a minority. Some churches have attempted to control the debate of congregational government using Robert's Rules of Order.[10] While this seems to be an appropriate impulse to bring structure to congregational discussions, here again the structure of the conversation and the decision-making process become so involved that it can become a hindrance to honest dialogue. A church that is pursuing revitalization will need to implement changes. A change process must be initiated and approved through the style of government the church has embraced. If there is not a clear understanding of the offices and decision-making structures of the church, then the revitalization process can be greatly hindered by competing groups within the church or confusion over how a change process could be implemented.

Developing Helpful Bylaws and Manuals

The key place where clear rules need to be written about the governance of the church is in the church bylaws. While it may seem like a tedious process to write, review, and edit bylaws, it is nevertheless necessary. A church may have well-written bylaws already. These will require review and potential discussion among the leadership and the church.[11] Often the church may operate on unwritten rules that conflict with the bylaws. The change process can be hindered when the church does not know who has authority and how that authority is executed. Beyond the bylaws, there will also need to be additional manuals that outline procedures within the church. These manuals need to be up to date, concise, and helpful. Church documentation should provide guidance, not cause paralysis.

Organization and Church Revitalization

It is often hard to know which comes first: a change of church leadership, organization, and culture, or a change toward revitalization that influences these areas. If a church is struggling with

---

10   Henry Roberts, et al., *Robert's Rules of Order in Brief* (New York: Public Affairs, 2020).
11   Robert Welch, *Church Administration: Creating Efficiency for Effective Ministry* (Nashville: B&H, 2011), 48–65.

revitalization, it is a sign that the leaders and leadership structure have not been able to respond to the opportunities and obstacles presented to the church in a way that produces thriving. Necessary change in this area is also difficult. When attempting to address the topic of church leadership and organization, the following advice is warranted.

First, a church cannot change that which it does not understand. Very often a church member is not fully aware of how a church operates. The average church member attends, meets with friends, notices aspects of the church that are important to him or her, and then goes on with the rest of his or her life. A measure of education will be important along with careful listening.

Second, church structure affects relationships. A pastor should be aware that if the church structure is changing, relational networks and potentially power networks will also change. A pastor will need to be sensitive to this reality. This is not an exercise in merely restructuring an organizational chart but may affect the way people have related to the church, which will create emotional angst. The leadership must manage the angst. If it is not managed, members can let personal reasons that do not have the ideal for the church in mind prevent needed change from occurring.

Third, a pastor must learn the unwritten rules and find areas where the old model of church structure was not enabling the church to meet ideals. An example of this may be pointing out that a partisan, majority-rule model is destroying church unity. Likewise, a pastor could point out that power is held too closely by one or two people, who lack needed accountability and transparency.

Fourth, when making changes it is important to address it patiently but strategically. Sometimes the church needs to know that the leaders can pause or stop if the congregation is at an emotional breaking point. Other times the church may be ready to make swift changes because members have embraced the new vision. In most situations, the leaders will be ready to make the change of leadership structure long before the church at large shares their level of enthusiasm.

What Does a Church Actually Do?

Many onlookers might merely see the church gather weekly for worship and believe that is the sole occurrence. The standing joke, which is quite hurtful to pastors, is the question of what they do outside the one day of the week they work. The church is a mysterious institution in which the matrices of success are not the same as in other organizations. Therefore, matrices for success must be set appropriately and in line with biblical principles. Acts 2:41–47 is a paradigm for the ministries of the church. While there is never a clear one-to-one correspondence between the book of Acts and the contemporary church, the basic ministries of preaching/teaching, fellowship, prayer, worship, ministry, and evangelism are clearly seen in this paradigmatic text.[12] While few pastors would take theological issue with the following list of church ministries, the actual lived practice of the church becomes more complicated. A church often takes on the personality of its leadership. On many occasions a church suffers from an imbalance of emphasis. It is not merely that a church must acknowledge a balanced offering of ministries, but a church must organize its schedule to reflect the theologically affirmed balance. Further, many questions about even the expression of these ministries must be answered in the life of the church.

Preaching and Teaching

The preaching event should be the main act of teaching in the local church. However, it cannot be the sole means of teaching if real learning and discipleship are to occur. The early church had both formal and informal teaching. There are many questions that need answering if teaching is to be done with intentionality. A major question is the nature of the recipient in the preaching event. Is the pastor preaching to believers or unbelievers? While on one level preaching is for everyone, there needs to be intentionality about whether the primary focus is on believers or unbelievers. This focus will adjust the nature of the preaching event. There are many other questions

---

12 John Stott, *The Message of Acts* (Downers Grove, IL: InterVarsity, 1990), 81–87.

to be worked through regarding preaching. If a pastor is going to lead revitalization in the church, there will be many more tasks to complete outside preaching and preparation. Some pastors commit up to twenty hours a week in preparation for preaching. While this is a noble objective, it requires evaluation considering other areas of pastoral care and leadership that will also need attention. Sadly, in many churches the demands of the pastor are more related to pastoral care and church administration than to preaching.

Many in the congregation will make demands of the pastor regarding pastoral care needs or tending to church-administration issues. Rarely will a church member chastise the pastor for a failure to spend hours in the study preparing to preach. The pastor will need to craft and implement a plan for preparation. This could be done by communicating office hours to the congregation that are set apart for sermon preparation. The pastor will need to guard the time for preparation along with communicating to the church when the issues of pastoral care and administration can be addressed as well. Preaching will not merely be teaching the Bible. The preaching event is a time to lead the church as well.[13] This can be accomplished through a pre-introduction to the message that communicates church vision or through a message series that drives home key elements of church renewal. Utilizing the message to single out or rebuke church members, even in the interest of driving home key elements of church renewal, should not be done. If confrontation is needed, it should occur in private and not indirectly while preaching. A pastor will need to think through what enables the greatest learning in the church, and will need to weigh the options of expository, topical, or an eclectic style of preaching. While there is much to be commended about expository preaching,[14] many churches have endured overly long message series through books of the Bible that do not seem to be conducive to learning. Topical

---

13   William Willimon, *Leading with the Sermon: Preaching as Leadership* (Minneapolis: Fortress, 2020).
14   Wayne McDill, *12 Essential Skills for Great Preaching* (Nashville: B&H, 2006).

messages can be helpful when the topic is truly biblically evaluated and communicated. Further, learning to preach in a narrative way can be effective in a culture that enjoys stories.[15] Since the church will listen to a pastor on a regular basis, freshness is important. The pastor will need to work hard not only on the content of the preaching event but also on the form and presentation of preaching to enable the congregation to engage. While many pastors feel inadequate, the Holy Spirit is active in the communication of God's Word. While pastors should study to be approved (2 Tim. 2:15), the Holy Spirit is ultimately the person who opens minds and hearts to be receptive to truth (Heb. 3:15).[16]

While so many pastors focus time and energy on the preaching event, there is a great deal more teaching to do than preaching. For a church to be revitalized it must have a robust discipleship process, which will require teaching. The essence of the term *disciple* is "learner." Learning must occur formally and informally. Groups in some form will need to have a central place in the structure of the church. This can still be accomplished by traditional Sunday school classes or small groups either on or off campus. There needs to be real leadership in this area. Some church leaders give much time and attention to preaching in the corporate worship service only to let the educational ministries of the church float adrift without appropriate direction. Part of the pastor's task is to teach the teachers of the church. The church will need to constantly recruit and train new teachers. Further, there are many approaches to group organization. Groups can be organized to merely discuss and apply the contents of a pastor's message. Or they can center on teaching curriculum or the interest of the group. Groups can also be organized around a teacher from whom many want to glean information. Again, there is no one-size-fits-all strategy for groups other than the importance of

---

15 Calvin Miller, *Preaching: The Art of Narrative Exposition* (Grand Rapids: Baker Books), 2006.

16 Greg Heisler, *Spirit-Led Preaching: The Holy Spirit's Role in Sermon Preparation and Delivery* (Nashville: B&H, 2018).

having the church connected into groups for the purpose of learning, deepening discipleship, fellowship, and outreach.[17] Groups can be a great aid when leading a revitalization. If many groups within the church can catch the vision of church revitalization and communicate it in a more intimate setting, the church will likely develop momentum. One word of caution: the leadership should not be surprised if long-standing groups are resistant to church revitalization. This does not necessarily mean that a long-standing group will forever be resistant to a particular vision of church revitalization; it likely means that this group has weathered many storms in this church. This group has developed a way to survive in less-than-ideal situations within the church. These groups, however, can become some of the most faithful supporters if the leadership team is able to win them over. Resistant people are resistant for a reason, and a true leader will attempt to understand the nature of the resistance. A test of leadership will be how a church revitalizer deals with resistance to change within the church from many arenas.

Christian Fellowship

The nature of Christian fellowship is crucial to church health. If a church does not experience life together in some meaningful way, then it will be difficult for church health and vitality to occur. Churches can either encourage or discourage appropriate fellowship with the way the church calendar is scheduled. An overscheduled church can so fixate the congregation on the church building that in the context of busyness, genuine fellowship is suffocated. On the other hand, appropriate scheduling, or encouragement of certain activities by the church, can bring about the context for genuine fellowship. For example, encouraging members to invite people to their homes and get to know new people

---

17   Chris Surratt, *Leading Small Groups: How to Gather, Launch, Lead and Multiply Your Small Group* (Nashville: B&H, 2019). While there is good information concerning small groups in many church settings, a traditional Sunday school is workable and effective. The convenience of meeting in the church building with provided childcare is often more attractive than meeting in homes. Each church must evaluate its own situation.

can be a scheduled event that facilitates real fellowship.[18] The early Christians enjoyed having meals with one another, and modern-day Christians could deeply benefit from the simple joy of a shared meal. Proximity to other believers within the church is important for genuine fellowship. The rise of the worship-service event has encouraged many to drive quite a distance from their home to attend a worship service. This may be necessary in some cases, but it is not ideal. To live, work, and worship in proximity to one's home is ideal for discipleship. Larger churches that have a greater reach attempt to address this through satellite campuses or dispersed groups. These have proved effective in some contexts. In church revitalization, wrongly conceived church fellowship can often lead to inward thinking and be perceived as a hindrance to revitalization. While there is some truth in this, the development of robust community is actually a very positive tool for attracting outsiders. People are looking for real community, and if that can be developed within a church, it will naturally attract those outside the church. If there is a sense of community within the church, but the nature of that community is not spiritually and emotionally healthy, then intentionally addressing this with patience and understanding may likely be a pastor's first task in revitalization. This unhealthy fellowship is likely the result of poor family systems and broken relationships, and provides an opportunity for understanding, forgiveness, reconciliation, and renewed trust. As a result, those from outside the church will be able to enter a healthier situation. The leadership team must often realize that the task of revitalization and renewal must first take place in the hearts of those who are there before it will spread into the community. Rather than seeing unhealthy people within the church as an obstacle to revitalization, leadership must recognize that these people are likely the first God-given opportunity for renewal. If renewal cannot happen to those who are within the church, how is the minister to expect it will happen to those without the church?

---

18 Rosaria Butterfield, *The Gospel Comes with a House Key* (Wheaton, IL: Crossway, 2018). Butterfield gives a compelling story of conversion due to the simplicity of hospitality and genuine Christian fellowship.

Worship and Prayer

Worship is described in the Bible as a way of life, an all-encompassing approach to one's Christian life.[19] While it is right and good to think about worship in this way, the church also gathers for corporate worship. It is certainly wrong to think that the shape and style of corporate worship will not affect the way a Christian approaches worship as a way of life. Corporate worship will need to be reflected on so that it is a true aid for Christians to lead a life of worship. There are so many factors that affect the worship service. While it is appropriate for corporate worship to be primarily for the building up of believers, many nonbelievers will also attend. Pastors should cultivate an awareness that nonbelievers and/or new Christians attend corporate worship as well. Churches can love their neighbors in corporate worship by merely extending a genuine welcome to non-Christians who attend. Too many churches simply do not think about their church as the outsider experiences it. Simple acts of thoughtfulness should include:

- an up-to-date webpage with directions,
- clear signage that the outsider has arrived at the church property,
- greeters to guide attenders into the building and signage within the building to guide movement,
- a clearly devised safety and security policy so parents are comfortable with dropping off their children, and
- a welcoming environment that does not put new people on the spot.

Further, insider language should be avoided wherever possible to make the general experience of the church intelligible. The church building itself communicates how the congregation feels about its worship. Any building can be cleaned and maintained with some level

19   David Peterson, *Engaging with God: A Biblical Theology of Worship* (Downers Grove, IL: InterVarsity, 1992), 283–88.

of competency. A dirty or poorly maintained building communicates to guests how they view the importance of corporate worship.

Once corporate worship begins there are specific elements that should be considered. All areas of corporate worship—praying, preaching, singing, financial giving, baptism, the Lord's Supper, congregational response—require investigation. Prayer, a central element of the Christian faith, is often treated very cursorily in corporate worship services. The death of the corporate prayer meeting is commonplace in the American church. A time for dedicated prayer in the main corporate worship service is lacking. Singing in worship has been fraught with challenges. The push and pull between liturgical, traditional, contemporary, and blended worship styles seems to have no end. Music is simply very important to many people who attend church. A worship pastor has a complex job. A failure to appreciate the complexity and nuance of this struggle will not bode well for the church. A worship pastor must be able to listen, collaborate, and communicate gracefully regarding theological principles in worship. Music can be used to soften people's hearts and attune their minds and hearts to God. A music ministry that is devoid of this ability to cultivate a worshipful context is missing something. On the other hand, when the singing event becomes the sole focus of the worship service, something has gone wrong and attunement to God is likely not what is occurring. A church will need to be realistic about acceptable styles of music, a realistic assessment of musical talent, and the ability or lack thereof for paid staff to aid with music.[20]

Financial giving is an act of worship. It is also a vital resource for the ministries of the church and should be given a place in worship. Financial giving often occurs in the middle of a worship service when the offering plate is passed. In some church contexts, this makes the

20   Paul Engle and Paul Basden, eds., *Exploring the Worship Spectrum: Six Views* (Grand Rapids: Zondervan, 2004). Books that review the spectrums of options for the nature of corporate worship can enable church leaders to think through the issues related to corporate worship from more than one perspective. It seems that diversity of style and intentionality have the best chance to aid in the communication of divine truth.

congregation uncomfortable or feels outdated. For greater discretion, some churches merely allow for opportunities before or after the worship service to gather the offering. Many church members now primarily give their offering online. Clear teaching about financial giving is needed. There is much theological debate over whether giving 10 percent is a hard-and-fast biblical principle. The teaching of the New Testament appears to affirm that giving is based upon several principles, not a mere percentage.[21] However, there is no genuine theological argument against the mandate for giving to support the needs of the church. Giving requires the church to have not only theological convictions on the nature of giving in the life of the Christian but also clearly devised financial practices that protect the financial integrity of the church. A scandal in financial management will do considerable harm to the reputation of the church. From the moment monies are collected, to the process of counting, depositing, bookkeeping, and allocating funds to be spent, the church needs a clearly devised process replete with checks and balances. If a church begins to grow and more money is received, older models that pro-tected the church at one level of giving may not be able to maintain integrity as bookkeeping becomes more complex. The church needs to have some level of transparency regarding how money is spent. A budget with expenses ought to be made available to the congregation at some point within the calendar year. Another struggle for church members in giving is clarity on where to give. Older churches have many specific designated funds where money can be given outside the general fund. While it can be helpful for people to designate their money to a particular area, this can also create problems for the church. A church member can give money to specific projects while neglecting the day-to-day operations of the church. It is possible for a church to have many restricted funds that have money and struggle

---

21   David Croteau, *You Mean I Don't Have to Tithe? A Deconstruction of Tithing and a Reconstruction of Post-tithe Giving* (Eugene, OR: Pickwick, 2010). Cro-teau makes a compelling case that the New Testament moves beyond a fixed percentage to principles that should encourage greater generosity.

to maintain day-to-day expenses. If a church has additional funds to allocate, a clear rationale needs to be established on why this will be helpful to the mission of the church.[22]

Baptism and the Lord's Supper are at times thought of as secondary in corporate worship.[23] This should not be the case. The health of a church is often seen in the frequency of baptism. Even in these areas there is a robust theological debate. A church will need to clearly articulate what it believes about baptism and the Lord's Supper. A pastor should not assume that these ordinances are understood, or their significance rightly absorbed in the minds of the church members. It is commonplace for those participating in baptism to believe it has a saving quality, and many partaking in the Lord's Supper are often confused as to what they are supposed to be doing other than remaining somber. Clear teaching will be required for these ordinances to be understood within a denominational tradition. Further, these ordinances ought to be practiced frequently enough that they are understood as key aspects of Christian worship.

Evangelism

Evangelism is a major aspect of church life. The gospel is central in the life of the Christian and the church. The church is founded upon the gospel. Therefore, the ability to clearly articulate the gospel is a skill that every Christian needs. The articulation of the gospel requires more than mere skill. God uses human agency in his larger purposes of bringing people to salvation. A church should actively share the gospel with the lost, while trusting in God's power to work in the hearts and lives of people. Gospel-sharing in an increasingly

---

22 Jamie Dunlop, *Budgeting for a Healthy Church: Aligning Finances with Biblical Priorities for Ministry* (Grand Rapids: Zondervan, 2019). Dunlop reviews the various areas that need to be thought through when devising a quality budget.

23 On baptism see G. R. Beasley-Murray, *Baptism in the New Testament* (Grand Rapids: Eerdmans, 1962). Beasley-Murray has written a definitive work on the nature of baptism in the New Testament. On the Lord's Supper see Thomas Schreiner and Matthew Crawford, eds., *The Lord's Supper: Remembering and Proclaiming Christ until He Comes* (Nashville: B&H, 2010), 264–390.

post-Christian world is requiring thinking like missionaries even in
our own communities.[24] The culture will not necessarily share our
presuppositions about belief in God, the reality of sin, and the need
for salvation. Indeed, they may seem foreign. Evangelism strategies
may therefore need to be adjusted to account for this reality, but
God is still able to work through obedient Christians who desire to
faithfully share the gospel with others. The church would be wise to
give clear education on ways to faithfully present the gospel and offer
opportunities for evangelistic engagement.

ARE WE MAKING DISCIPLES WHO MAKE DISCIPLES?

The core mandate of the local church is to make disciples who will
make disciples. While many churches have this goal in their mission
statement, the struggle to make genuine disciple-making a reality in
the life of the church requires great intentionality. While discipleship
is a noble aspiration, the church will need to devise an approach to
discipleship that is clearer than the aspirational goal. Many churches
do not make this move from aspirational goals to a clear approach
to making disciples.

There are several broad approaches to making disciples. These
approaches could be described as educational models, relational
models, developmental models, and ministry/evangelism models.[25]
Educational models of discipleship focus on learning. This is rightly
emphasized: the simple definition of the word *disciple* is "learner."
To be rightly understood, the Christian faith requires learning. This
approach to discipleship clarifies a certain body of teaching that needs
to be reviewed by the person seeking discipleship. This approach could
be limited in duration so that the church guided all their new disciples

---

24 Sam Chan, *Evangelism in a Skeptical World: How to Make the Unbelievable
    News about Jesus More Believable* (Grand Rapids: Zondervan, 2018). Chan is
    commended for attempting to set forth a framework for gospel sharing in a
    post-Christian era.
25 George Barna, *Growing True Disciples: New Strategies for Producing Genuine
    Followers of Christ* (Colorado Springs: WaterBrook, 2001), 133–60.

through a finite amount of curriculum. Or it could be open-ended, the church teaching in various forms that drive the discipleship process. The fact that Jesus taught within the context of relationship highlights the need for a relational approach to the discipleship process. While the focus of the educational approach to discipleship is on the teacher, the relational approach focuses on the cooperation of the relationship. While there will be a leader within the group, the manner of the group and the nature of teaching within the group will feel different. The teaching will often be more personalized to the individuals in the group. This can be accomplished by establishing smaller groups, either co-ed or separated by gender, which serve as the crucible of discipleship.

The developmental model is attuned to the reality that every disciple is at a different spiritual stage and life-cycle stage.[26] The discipleship plan needs to be tailored accordingly. A widowed woman in her seventies will not benefit from a class on biblical parenting. For this tailoring to happen, some form of assessment is needed to discern the spiritual stage of the person. This requires the church to have a clear process of evaluation for its church members, and it requires church members who are willing to receive some level of evaluation. The church must think through how it will communicate to those who rate low in spiritual maturity without creating tension. This level of assessment can be helpful if done in a tactful way.

If the goal of making disciples is for the discipled to become the discipler, then a plan for launching disciples needs to be implemented. Discipleship can become overly inward, but the goal is for it to be outward and expanding. Part of the discipleship process should enable a person to find their area of service and use their talents to the glory of God. This discernment of spiritual gifts, talents, and callings is an important aspect of becoming a disciple, which propels the disciple outward into service. Further, a discipled person should be

---

26 Jim Putnam, *Real-Life Discipleship: Building Churches That Make Disciples* (Colorado Springs: NavPress, 2010). Putnam organizes his entire discipleship program around a developmental or lifestyle model.

able to develop spiritual confidence to share their faith. A clear plan for evangelism should be implemented in the church. The simple use of a gospel tract as a guide can be very helpful for many. However, this can also feel too templated and simplistic in a pluralistic culture. Relational approaches to sharing the gospel can be taught with the role of personal testimony and biblical storytelling. A disciple can progress to the point where they know many evangelism approaches and are able to utilize the best approach for the moment.

If deep revitalization in a church is going to happen, then deep change and discipleship will need to occur in the members of the church. A church needs a plan for discipleship, but the church must likewise be careful that the plan does not get in the way of genuine, organic discipleship. The structure and program for discipleship needs to allow for some level of personalization. For example, some churches focus on family discipleship as their preferred method for discipleship. The material and organization help families engage with one another. However, churches can unwittingly alienate singles by focusing the discipleship process too narrowly. This is where the pastoral leadership in the church needs to balance the structure of a discipleship plan with the needs of the members. The combination of pastoral sensitivity to church members' personal situations within the context of a thoughtful plan allows for genuine discipleship to occur. Ultimately, discipleship works best when there is quality connection between two or more people who engage with one another to live out the commands of Jesus. A discipleship process should create a positive environment in which rich, relational connections can be made that have greater Christlikeness as their goal.[27] Revitalization begins within the heart of church members, and this occurs as they deepen their relationship with God.

---

27 Michael Wilkins, *Following the Master: A Biblical Theology of Discipleship* (Grand Rapids: Zondervan, 1992). Wilkins attempts to trace the theme of discipleship across the New Testament in an attempt to develop a more comprehensive vision of discipleship.

WHAT MINISTRY? HOW MUCH MINISTRY?

Church revitalization will require leadership. This alone takes a great deal of time in addition to the weekly rhythm of preaching. However, many in the church look to the pastor or a pastoral staff team as ministers. This implies to the church that pastors are out among their flock ministering, not merely leading or teaching. A failure to appropriately minister to the church will harm a pastor's ability to lead and even be heard while preaching. Pastoral burnout is a reality, so care must be taken when thinking through the need for balance and wisdom in these areas. In smaller and even medium-sized churches, the pastor is still expected to have a visitation program. This may seem disconnected from revitalization but winning the confidence of the congregation and being there in pastoral care situations is very important to be able to lead change within the church.

The Task of Congregational Care

Visitation is a one-on-one event. Therefore, those within the church do not know who is being visited by the pastor. Also, there are certainly groups that the church may see as especially important to be visited by a pastor. These include those in the hospital, shut-ins, and the elderly. It can be helpful for the pastor to publicize his visitation plan. This way the church can have confidence that a visitation program is in place and will not allow for the accusation that no visitation is happening. Also, many may want more attention from the pastor than what is being given. Communication in this area is of the uttermost importance. If there are sixty members within the church who should receive visits from the pastor, and the pastor spends one day a week on visitation, then he can implement the expectation that he will only be able to visit them four or five times a year. This apparent lack of visitation may seem more reasonable when they are aware of the amount of people and the process for visiting them.

Further, a pastor will need to set up a communication system for needs within the church to be funneled to appropriate channels. The assumption can too often be that the pastoral staff is aware of all the church's needs. Whether through online or written documentation, the congregation needs to be educated on how to make requests to pastoral staff. Otherwise, some in the congregation may assume the pastor knows about their situation and then seek to harm his reputation when he does not visit. A clear process for submitting requests to the pastor can facilitate information and protect the pastor against these types of accusations. If requests are made but not followed up on, then a pastor needs a better system. If requests are not made, then the congregation may need to be reeducated on how to request a pastoral visit.

Pastors are expected to preside over weddings and funerals. These are pivotal events in a person's life. Again, these responsibilities may be understood as separate from leading revitalization, but they are not. Being present at joyous and sorrowful moments in people's lives gives a pastor credibility to lead the church. Until the pastor has ministered in these moments, he likely does not have the confidence of the church to lead them in other areas. These areas also have pitfalls. A clearly devised and communicated plan for marriage ceremonies needs to be expressed to the church. It should be known publicly under what conditions a minister is willing to marry a couple. This likely needs to be part of what the pastor tells the group that hires him. A pastor's unexpected refusal to perform marriage ceremonies for certain persons will likely create rifts in the church. While convictions are important, it is likewise important to communicate these convictions early. Rifts in the church hinder the process of revitalization.

Funerals are important events. They create a unique opportunity to meet the extended families of church members. Positive interactions and care expressed in these moments can win a great deal of goodwill for pastor and church alike.

The pastor should participate in caring for the needs of the church but should not attempt to do all care of the church.[28] It is precisely at this place that groups or Sunday school classes, serving deacons, and ministering teams or committees can perform great care in the

---

28 Harold Senkbeil, *The Care of Souls: Cultivating a Pastor's Heart* (Bellingham, WA: Lexham, 2019).

church. Care within a church will take structures, communication channels, and processes. This process of setting up a care structure is hard work. However, much harder work is entailed when no care structure is in place. If a pastor does not have the skill set to set up a process like this, then assistance should be sought from someone gifted in this area within the church. There are many venues for accomplishing outcomes of care, such as care within groups, deacons who are responsible for certain sections of the congregation, and ministries that focus on a vulnerable group. These structures need to grow around the needs of the church so that care is appropriately given. A pastoral staff can truly maximize their pastoral presence by making initial contact with needs within the church but then shifting these needs to more robust ministries that can devote more time and attention to their specific needs.

Community Ministry

To experience revitalization, a church will need to express ministry beyond the walls of the church. However, the people within the church have needs that require ministry as well. Ideally, as church members mature, they need less ministry and can offer more ministry to others. This ideal takes time to develop, so patience is needed. Leading revitalization and attempting to develop ministries just to care for those present within the church requires a great deal of focus. The implementation of children's ministry, youth ministries, singles ministry, men's ministry, women's ministry, family ministries, and senior adult ministries is multilayered and time-intensive. In the age of personalization, church members are unfortunately looking for a church that meets their needs rather than attempting to meet the needs of the church. Again, a pastor should not succumb to the desire for overpersonalization of the church experience to the neglect of genuine community. Yet the pastor cannot forget that this is the culture we live in and to be missional even with his own members and offer some level of appropriate contextualization.

It is easy to see why outreach is lacking in many churches. Keeping the internal operations of a church going, especially with limited pastoral staff, is no small task. However, for revitalization to occur more must be done than quality internal operations. The pastoral staff, church leaders, and church cannot and should not settle for this. To experience revitalization, the church must simultaneously produce an internal plan for pastoral care while reaching into the community. Community engagement will take different shapes depending on the nature of the community around the church. This is where contextualization is so important. The church will need to engage the community in ways that the community can value the church's contribution. This engagement could be event-based, relational, and/or based on an ongoing program or ministry. A church will struggle to revitalize if it does not have a community presence. It could be insightful for church members to merely interview the non-churched neighbors around the church neighborhood to see what their impression of the church is. Often churches are surprised by their community's perception of them. This vision of the church as understood by the members should be communicated and lived out in such a way that bystanders are able to see the good that the church is doing.

Ministries like food assistance, clothing assistance, temporary housing, and counseling assistance are welcomed in many communities. Not every church has the budget for these ministries, but many in the culture look especially to the church to provide them. Again, the reason that many churches struggle to make these external ministries thrive is because the demands of those within the church are so great that ministry struggles to reach outside the group. If these types of ministries that reach outside the church are going to flourish, then organization will be critical. If mercy ministries like these are going to occur, who will lead them? In smaller churches, these ministries will need to be volunteer-led. In larger churches, pastoral staff can oversee these ministries. If ministries reach a certain size, they often become too unwieldy for volunteers alone and paid staff must assist. It is at this point that parachurch or other nonprofit organizations can help. Whole organizations can exist for food distribution or clothes distribution. There are organizations that take in the homeless and provide counseling assistance. A church may decide merely to provide support to these organizations and can minister to their communities with the aid of other organizations. Even in this there is a caution. Parachurch organizations can open the door to influence and move from assisting the church in ministry to dictating and draining the church of people and resources. Balance must be maintained in this area.

The Role of Mission Beyond the Community

While a church is focused on its community, it should also remember the nations of the world. Local community ministry should spur great mission to places outside one's community. It is ideal for a church to work with a mission organization and invest in mission initiatives outside the local community. Taking people to the wider mission field can open their eyes to the larger global need. The church's focus on the nations can enable it to rightly focus less on itself and more on the need that exists in the world. The call to mission work is a needed aspect of discipleship. If a church is faithfully ministering to its community and in an international mission scene, the spirit of revitalization is already being manifested in these activities.

Funding the Ministry

Last, a church will need to make a budgetary decision. How much money or what percentage of the budget will be spent on direct ministry into the community, and how much will be spent on missions? It can be strange when churches state that they are focused on ministering to people and to the wider mission, but their budget tells a different story. The budget is consumed with personnel and building expenses, with a rather small percentage on direct community ministry and missions. While pastoral staff are often underpaid and need appropriate compensation and a building requires maintenance, the need for real investment in ministry and mission is important. A rule to guide a church could be 30 percent personnel, 30 percent building, 30 percent ministry, and 10 percent missions. In smaller churches the personnel expense will likely be higher than 30 percent, but attention must be given to funding and supporting the critical functions of ministry and missions. When the spirit of ministry and the heart of missions are born in a church, church revitalization will likely not be far behind. The church should make sure that plenty of giving opportunities are provided to the church and intentionality is present in ministry funding.[29]

Addressing the Building

While the church is not a building, a pastor will need a clear-eyed vision for the place of the building in the overall philosophy of church life. Many pastors in a revitalization situation inherit a building with years of deferred maintenance. While building or entering a capital improvement plan will not bring about revitalization, sometimes attention to the building is necessary to move the church forward. Years of deferred maintenance give a clear visual that the church is in decline. A clean, updated building gives the impression that the ministry is well maintained. Addressing the building will require expertise in construction, renovation, budgeting, and capital improvement planning. Leadership with these skill sets will need to be discovered to make sure that building maintenance does not become a hindrance rather than a help to the efforts of church revitalization. When needs are many and money is tight, careful planning and execution of the most pressing needs must be carefully planned. However, ignoring the issue of the building will likely not be an option either. So careful movement toward addressing building issues will be necessary.

Stating Your Convictions

Before launching out into church revitalization, it is important to know one's convictions about the life of the church. These convictions are theological and methodological. Theological convictions must be established so that the church is faithful to the witness of the Scriptures and is consistent with the life of the church through

---

29 Nelson Searcy, *Maximize: How to Develop Extravagant Givers in Your Church* (Grand Rapids: Baker Books, 2010). Searcy gives clear guidance on how to encourage people to greater generosity.

church history. Methodological convictions must be established so that the type of church that emerges out of the crucible is not a surprise to the church leaders. Clearly thinking through and stating one's conviction ahead of time creates the foundation on which an intentional church-revitalization effect can be established.

STATING YOUR CONVICTIONS

Denominational Affiliation

- ○ No denomination
- ○ Embracing a denomination (specify _____)
- ○ Embracing a doctrinal statement (specify _____)

Elders and Pastoral Staff

- ○ Primarily elder-led church
- ○ Primarily staff-led church
- ○ Primarily pastor-led church
- ○ Primarily congregationally led church
- ○ Primarily denominationally led church

The Role of Deacons

- ○ Church administration and practical ministry oversight
- ○ Practical ministry oversight only

Church Membership

- ○ No church membership
- ○ Low-commitment membership
- ○ High-commitment members

STATING YOUR CONVICTIONS

Preaching and Teaching

O Primarily expository

O Primarily topical

O Eclectic style (specific _____)

Fellowship

O Primarily organic fellowship

O Primarily planned fellowship opportunities

O Primarily programmed fellowship

Worship

O Primarily focused on accommodation of nonbelievers

O Primarily focused on building up believers

Which aspects will be regularly part of corporate worship?

O Prayer (how frequent in worship?) _____

O Baptism (what mode/meaning?) _____

O Lord's Supper (what meaning/frequency?) _____

O Giving (What means of giving? Collection plate, online, etc.?) _____

O Preaching (How prominent in service? Length of time?) _____

O Music (What style? Traditional? Contemporary? Liturgical? Blended?) _____

O Other _____

STATING YOUR CONVICTIONS

Prayer

- O A regularly scheduled time for corporate prayer
- O Specific times of called corporate prayer
- O Prayer dispersed throughout ministries

Evangelism

- O A planned evangelistic program
- O A taught evangelistic approach
- O No formal evangelistic program

Disciple-Making Plan

- O Educational model
- O Relational model
- O Developmental model
- O Ministry/evangelism model
- O Other (specify _____)

Congregational Care

- O Congregational care (primarily pastoral responsibility)
- O Congregational care (primarily deacon responsibility)
- O Congregational care (primarily groups responsibility)

Church Ministry Programming

- O Very programmed church
- O Moderately programmed church
- O Low-programmed church

STATING YOUR CONVICTIONS

Community Involvement

- O Community ministry through attractional events
- O Community ministry through community-based programs
- O Community ministry through organic relationships
- O Community ministry through mercy ministries
- O Community ministry through parachurch partnership
- O Other _____

Missions Involvement

- O Intentional mission involvement primarily through mission trips
- O Intentional missional involvement primarily through giving
- O Intentional missional involvement primarily through prayer and education
- O No intentional mission involvement

Funding Strategy (What Percentage of Budget per Area?)

- O Staff (_____%)
- O Building (_____%)
- O Ministries (_____%)
- O Missions (_____%)

Building

- O The building is very important
- O The building is somewhat important
- O The building is not important

CHAPTER 3

CHARTING A CHURCH'S HISTORY

Amajor difference between a church revitalizer and a church planter is that a church that needs to be revitalized has a history. The history of the church is not mere fact. That history has established patterns of thought and behavior that are affecting the church now.[1] Further, if the church has a long history, such as more than one hundred years, it is possible that unless copious records were taken and the history often repeated to the congregation, the history has been forgotten. Church leaders must not just minister to the church that is currently gathered without understanding the church that has gathered in the past.

WRITING A BRIEF CHURCH HISTORY

Understanding a church's history can be simply done by writing a brief history. In some churches, a history of the church has already been written. This is an invaluable resource for understanding the history of the church. The reason for understanding the history of

---

1   Edwin Friedman, *Generation to Generation: Family Process in Church and Synagogue* (New York: Guilford, 1985), 193–219.

the church is different from merely stating information and creating a timeline. It will be important that the timeline church leadership creates is accurate and gathers sufficient evidence to avoid distortion of the church's history. Depending on the vitality and longevity of the church, the history can likely be divided into ten-year increments. Another straightforward way to divide the church in eras is through the terms of each pastorate. This alone is an interesting organizing principle because this will visually show the length of each pastorate. If a pastor comes into a church expecting to have a long pastorate and the average tenure of a pastor is three or four years, then that aspect of the church's history will likely repeat itself.

Writing this history will be important for church leadership. Church leaders must learn to embrace the church that is there and the story of the church that has already happened. Coming into the church without clarity about its difficulties will likely make any church leadership planning fail to resonate with the story they have experienced over many years. Further, the church needs to know that church leaders are willing to embrace what has been before they forge ahead into what they believe the church should become. The language, the stories, the successes, and the controversies of the past will color any plan that church leadership sets forth. Therefore, knowing and digesting the history of the church is a worthy effort.

Data Required to Write a Church History				
Assessing Past Pastorates	Reviewing Church Records	Reviewing Major Decisions	Reviewing Spiritual Successes	Carefully Listening to Church Members and Community

Assessing Past Pastorates

It is possible to attempt revitalization with unrealistic goals. Church leaders should never cease to believe that the God who raises the dead can bring new life into a church. Yet leaders should have wisdom on the course of action and reasonable expectations for the church now. It can be sobering to study the pastorates of the past. If a former pastor is alive, it is invaluable to be able to discuss his pastorate with him. While charting the church's history, each pastor is added to the timeline with a simple summary of the former pastor's successes and failures; it is sobering to see how little or how much is accomplished in one pastorate. Many pastorates in American churches are brief; the average hovers around four years. If a pastorate is charted out into phases, the first year is often the honeymoon period. The church is happy to receive a new pastor. A pastor is typically not faced with making major changes in this first year. If a pastor does try to do something major within this first year, then it may result in a noticeably short pastorate. The second year a pastor can see opportunities for change and is beginning to be viewed by the congregation as the leader. The changes attempted in this second year are important. If mistakes are made in the second year, then conflict arises in the church. Then there can be a season of latency or conflict that drags into year three. If the pastor gets too conflicted or is frustrated by year four, the pastor often moves on to another ministry or steps out of ministry for a season. This is a common pattern. If a pastor has "wins" in the early years, then around year five is when the changes within the church really begin to change church culture. The pastor who can weather through difficult seasons and establish a long-term pastorate will be more successful.

When writing a church's history, a pastor needs the humility to embrace the fact that his pastorate will likely face challenges similar to the pastorates of the past. He will likely not have any greater accomplishments than previous pastors unless he makes significant changes in how church opportunities and obstacles are managed. A pastor can feel better about what he is able to attempt when deeply internalizing the past accomplishments and struggles of previous pastors. He can feel as though he is not alone in this struggle to change the church. However, realizing that these obstacles that have persisted over years or even decades can provide needed perspective.

Reviewing Church Records

The church history that is written is only as good as the objective data that the history rests on. There are some key documents that need to be accessed so that the history is written accurately. Even if a church has kept poor records, often a few key records are present. Most churches faithfully record attendance and budget. While many in the church keep a close eye on the budget and attendance numbers week to week, often a church does not step back and notice larger budget or attendance trends. For example, a slowly declining attendance may be noticed but dismissed for various reasons. The congregation often does not wish to think about its church as in a state of decline. So various interpretations can be given when attendance slumps and then stabilizes. What could clearly be seen in a longer-term perspective as clear decline could be seen in the short term as mere fluctuation. It is important to plot the attendance on a graph that clearly displays overall trends of growth, stagnation, and decline.

The budget is another area where quality records are typically kept. If a church does not have quality records of its budget, then likely new church leadership will need to help the church perform an audit to make sure that there has been financial integrity. Here again a church is concerned about paying the next bill and supporting the current needs. Just like in many people's personal finances, money can be viewed in a very short-term way. A chart that helps the congregation see the overall financial trajectory of the church can be helpful. Some churches are resistant to thinking about finances as a major factor in church life. Church boards sometimes argue against adjusting church programs and decisions for financial reasons. While the church is certainly to be free from the love of money, keeping a clear eye on financial realities is necessary for the wise operation of a church. The sad reality is that many churches struggle to see the need for church revitalization clearly until the bank account is low or completely depleted. In some churches the first thing that church members are willing to embrace is the dire financial situation. Those who are reluctant to buy in to church change may initially buy in because they are able to see that financial change is needed. Also, a clear chart plotting out financial realities can help a church prepare ahead of time for future financial leanness that could be forecasted months before it happens. While a church history needs more than budget and attendance numbers, these are the most objective pieces of data that church leaders have that will serve to establish buy-in from more skeptical members who are more naturally resistant to change. Church leaders must also embrace the reality that no matter how clearly objective data is presented there are still some who will refuse to see it. This is not a failure of presentation or communication, but a deeply rooted mindset that is exceedingly difficult to change. Church leaders can only attempt to be as objective and clear as possible and move with those who are willing to face up to reality.

Reviewing Major Decisions

Official meeting minutes are another place to glean data. Often in established churches, there are mountains of records from meetings. The goal is to summarize the data to make it useful for planning in church revitalization. The attendance and giving charts that churches develop can be given more context when church meetings are reviewed in light of these objective points of data. For example, if a church had a successful period of giving and attendance, the minutes could be explored as to what decisions the church was making at that time that contributed to those moments. The same goes for periods of decline in giving and attendance.

Most people in the life of a church are aware the church has had seasons of difficulties, but often they have not thought through what might have been contributing factors to the seasons. If new church leadership can shed light on past opportunities and obstacles, this may be a means of developing rapport with key leaders within the church. Establishing cause and effect in the complexity of life situations is fraught with challenges. However, church leaders analyzing the history of a church could highlight, for instance, that every time the student ministry took a youth mission trip, attendance in the youth ministry rose for the following six months. Or that during years of increased attendance the number of ministries increased. Or that more people were discipled when new groups were added versus having a campaign to add more to the current groups. While again, the church may not agree with the analysis, setting a theory before the church of why the church of the past succeeded or struggled at least makes the congregation think in fresh ways about the church. There are certainly church interventions that seem to work in many different contexts. However, in many contexts it is often hard for people to see the success even when the data is plain to be seen. Here again, the goal is not primarily for a pastor to make the congregation see everything as he does. The goal is for church leaders to have a clear grasp on the shape of the church.

Reviewing Spiritual Successes

It would be wrong to merely wade through budget, attendance records, and church minutes to discover the health of a church. Hopefully, the church has recorded conversions, baptisms, mission opportunities, discipleship statistics, and so forth. It is especially important to notice the periods when the church was not merely bigger or richer but healthier. Sometimes bigger and richer means healthier, but not always. There could be seasons when the church was smaller with less means but engaged in more intentional disciple-making and outreach than in a period when it was larger.

Some churches fall into a state of decline because a strong season of mission, discipleship, and vitality leads to numerical growth and stronger financials. This vital generation may expand the physical campus, put the church in a strong financial situation, and set up the next generation for greater mission. However, this is not how it always goes. A new generation that has inherited a lot from an earlier, faithful generation can reap the numerical and financial benefits of a previous generation but have poor metrics of spiritual health. This is a hard revitalization to engage, but it is certainly possible for hard data to be positive, and the data of the church's spiritual health could be negative. If this is the case, then this contradiction would need to be revealed to the church to see if the congregation can be motivated to address it.[2]

---

2   Thom Rainer, *Autopsy of a Decreased Church: 12 Ways to Keep Yours Alive* (Nashville: B&H, 2014). Rainer points out critical areas of evaluation when attempting to understand the nature of church decline.

Solidifying Your Analysis

It is important when assessing the situation of a church that fresh analysis is performed. However, the fresh analysis of the leadership will need to be compared with the perception within the congregation. While it will be important to talk to the members of the church, often the members are not fully aware of the true state of the church. This is not to say that one should be dismissive of their perspective, but if the church needs revitalization, then strategic moves have not been made at the proper times to avoid the current situation. Church leaders must attempt an objective analysis of the full story and develop a current interpretation of the situation. This analysis is based on the data previously discussed. It is important to set up perimeters of the current reality of the church. Often in church-revitalization situations, the church is asked to weigh in on their understanding of the health of the church. This is important and has its place. However, if the congregation had fully realized the state of things, church revitalization would not be required. Therefore, before church leadership asks the church for input it is important to have a general understanding of the state of the church. Two major possibilities will appear when asking the congregation about the state of the church. On the one hand, the church could see the situation in a very clear-eyed manner yet not have the tools to move itself out of its current state. On the other hand, the church could fail to see the state of the church. Certainly, within every church there will be a variety of both, but discerning whether the church is ready to embrace revitalization will depend on whether a sizable group within the church currently sees the reality of the situation or, if they don't, whether they could with future education be brought along to see it. Church leadership should have a particularly good assessment of how clearly the congregation's perception of themselves is in line with the hard data that has been collected. If the distortion is great, then change will be much harder to accomplish.

Hearing the Church's Understanding of Its Situation

The congregation will always have its say. Therefore, bringing the congregation into the discussion about the church's current state and future vision in a proper way requires wisdom. Even if the congregation is blocked out of the visioning process, it will ultimately buy into the fresh vision or be resistant to it. The church needs to have an opportunity to speak into the process. Church leadership should be careful not to overextend or underutilize the church at large. The congregation likely does not want to feel the full weight of the problem and be burdened for solutions. If someone in the congregation has insight into problems with helpful solutions, then he or she likely needs to participate in supporting the leadership team. However, members of the congregation may not be able to develop a plan but are often willing to give their opinion on plans developed. While it is ideal that each congregational member be completely truthful to a leadership team, often anonymity helps members of the congregation to be more transparent about their feelings. Most church members do not wish to critique the church and asking for feedback that is not covered in anonymity will likely receive distorted results. Unfortunately, many just refuse to be transparent about their feelings when anonymity is lost.

Formal Surveys

Church members can give input through a formal survey. Many church consultants have developed church surveys. These church surveys typically analyze the church along major areas. These areas often include prayer, discipleship, evangelism, worship, fellowship, and ministry. The church is asked to rate these areas through questions or statements that are scored on a sliding scale. For example, if a congregant believes that the church is faithful to share the gospel, they will rate the church's faithfulness to gospel sharing on a scale from 1 to 10. The answers are compiled, and the church is provided with an assessment of its current state. Formal surveys can be helpful. They supply a structured process to glean data from the church at large. The data is less susceptible to skewing because of the structured process. It will likely be helpful for a church to give some version of a formal survey to a sample group within the congregation or to the entire congregation.

Overreliance on formal surveys will likely not enable the desired results. Often, church leaders have not done the challenging work discussed previously. Data has not been collected about the history of the church with diligence to understand as objectively as possible the current situation. Often, church leaders make a snap judgment about where the church is based on intuition without clear support- ing data. While passion is important in church revitalization, anger and frustration about the state of the church without clear data to support assumptions is very unhelpful to the process. Many church leaders have given formal surveys in hopes that the congregation will mirror their interpretation of the situation. Church leaders will need to see the formal survey as only one piece of data in the process, not the silver bullet to achieve crystal clarity on the state of things in the church.

Further, often congregational members will not be excited about taking a general assessment of the church, especially if there are press- ing needs that they believe need to be addressed immediately. Church leadership will need to contextualize the nature and rationale for the formal survey. If a survey is given with the hope that the congrega- tion will make plain the need for a staff member to be addressed or a ministry to be adjusted, then it will be important for a leadership team to start the process of addressing this pressing need separate from a general formal survey. The church may interpret such a move as passing the responsibility onto them to make a hard call. If there is a pressing situation, then it is likely that a churchwide survey will not be well received until that issue is addressed.

Formal surveys work best when the church is in decline without major pressing issues at the forefront of the minds of congregational members. If the congregation is unsure why the slump, then a formal survey can give a reasoned overview of the state of the church. This can lead to positive conversations about how areas of strength can be celebrated and how areas of growth can be addressed.[3]

---

3   Formal church surveys are available for purchase at https://churchanswers. com. This church survey is titled "Church Health Report."

The results of a formal survey can be helpful to church leadership but typically not in the way most think it will be. A formal survey typically does not tell an astute leadership team much they did not already know. However, the survey can reveal to the congregation things they did not realize collectively and supply a forum for new ways of thinking about and discussing church life. Also, processing through the results of the formal survey can allow church leadership to learn how the congregation thinks through issues. If the congregation is not willing to face up to realities or negative trends in the results, then the level of resistance to change can be assessed. Positively, a congregant may begin to see steps toward change and health and vocalize these changes when processing the survey results. This may give indication that initial steps can be taken with less resistance in the change process.

Often, a pastor should not expect to learn something major from a formal survey if he has done due diligence to get to know the congregation. If some major new insight is learned through a formal survey, church leaders should realize that they are out of touch with the church. The formal survey is not for church leaders to learn something new per se but for the congregation to have a tool to view their situation in fresh categories and supply a time to process the information, offering reflections on what the formal survey reveals. A formal survey is a good place to start a conversation but is merely breaking the ice in a longer change process. If church leaders believe giving a formal survey will make the congregation see their plight, accept the new ideas, and execute them swiftly, they are likely setting themselves up for disappointment.

Polling

Somewhere in the visioning process, congregational input will need to be gleaned. While a general survey can get the conversation started, it does not necessarily give clear direction on how the church feels about various changes. Polling the church is one simple way to get feedback on specific changes. While the church is ultimately driven by the direction of the Holy Spirit and wise leadership, it is unwise to attempt to enact changes without knowing where the congregation is on a particular matter. Some church leaders take the approach that they will enact change, lose all the members that disagree with their vision, and then rebuild from that point. While it is true that in some circumstances church members will leave the church because they disagree with the church's new vision, this can be mitigated with a more thoughtful process. Polling the church can help leaders get a clear picture of where the church is.

In a church that needs to be revitalized, there is often hidden resistance to even positive changes. If anonymity can be kept in conducting a church poll, then often a true representation as to those who will buy into the change and those who will resist the change will become clear. Often, when polls are conducted, church leaders are surprised by the amount of resistance present despite positive conversations regarding the nature of church obstacles and the need to overcome them. Church leadership should not be discouraged when reading the results of a church poll. This will merely help them set the proper pace of change in the church. Further, an unintended phenomenon can happen when the results of a church poll are published. If the polling issue is a reasonable recommendation and 20 percent of those polled resist change, then the remaining 80 percent of the church can express its bewilderment as to why some are resistant. This can help the resistant to see their minority status and encourage them to converse about their position with someone who vocally supported the recommendation. This allows the church to have difficult conversations and negates the requirement for church leadership to persuade every church member.

Informal Conversations

There is no substitute for one-on-one informal conversations with the church. Most churches that need revitalization are small enough that this must be done. People can and often do change their minds. Church leadership should not conclude that the first word from a congregational member is the last. Often, people must work through their initial emotions, have time to think about the church situation, and ponder the proposals to win the congregation's trust and approval. A church leader truly taking the time to meet face-to-face to listen and discuss the church situation is invaluable.

Sadly, in churches where the length of the pastorate is typically short, it has often been a significant time period since a minister had a face-to-face meeting to discuss the vision of the church. Many ministers have made pastoral connections with the church, but often ministers who are good at playing a chaplain role to their church are not skilled in expressing vision, while those who are good at expressing vision can be less skilled in sitting and listening to their congregation. The valuable conversation of listening and casting vision for what the church can be in the context of true dialogue can move resistant church members toward engagement. Church members respect a humble pastor who is willing to meet them face-to-face, listen, and lead them to brighter days. In these more personal situations, a pastor or church leader may be asked questions that require a prepared answer. A church member may press leadership about its commitment to the church. Resistance among some church members materializes because they can sense a pastor will leave the church if he does not receive approval on all proposals. There may be wisdom in the resistance of the church member to hold the status quo rather than allow an undercommitted pastor to start a change process and then leave. If this scenario has been part of the church's history, then the congregation knows the fallout of such scenarios. The period of change is a vulnerable period in the life of the church. A good surgeon does not start major surgery and then walk away in the middle because it is hard. A pastor and church leadership may need to express more than mere vision when meeting with those in the church. A pastor may specifically need to express his sincere heart for the church and his willingness to stick with the church through the process. This level of communication is difficult to achieve in a larger setting.

The informal conversation process is a required part of hearing from the church. One word of caution before entering this process: discussing church vision one-on-one can be an exhausting process. The same themes emerge over and over, and these conversations require vulnerability between both parties. A pastor will need to pace himself to avoid exhaustion. Further, a pastor and even other church leaders can become frustrated if these conversations are overscheduled. Four of these conversations a week is likely the most a pastor can perform on top of his other duties. Since he will need to be in a situation where a member within the congregation must work through emotions, a pastor will need to be in a place of emotional readiness for this experience. It is easy for a pastor to become impatient, insensitive, and frustrated if he is emotionally tired going into these conversations. Therefore, a pastor and other church leaders will need to be selective on how they approach people. Leaders in the church who have influence over sections of the church need to be prioritized so that others can begin advocating for change.

Voting or Affirmation Process

If a church affirms congregational government, then at some point in the visioning process you will need to ask the church for official approval. If a church does not embrace a congregational form of government, it is still important to receive some level of affirmation before entering a season of revitalization. There are avenues of performing a churchwide vote that can either help or harm the process.

A mere majority voting system will not likely result in the desired buy-in necessary for real change. If the church realizes that only 51 percent is required to effect change, then this limits the need for collaboration between various groups within the church. If change is only supported by a narrow majority of the church, this is not sufficient for real change. Once a group within the church feels as though they have lost, they can become demotivated to embrace the change or they might form a group of resistance. These actions can be manifested in very immature ways. However, a wise pastor needs to understand the realities of sinful hearts and the power of wounded emotions.

It is ideal if a process of congregational approval can be established that aids greater buy-in and dialogue among various groups within the church. For example, the threshold for passing a needed change could be raised. Rather than mere majority rule, it might help to make a higher percentage of the church (such as 75 percent) required for a recommended change to be implemented.

It is precisely at this point that an attempt at church unity needs to be strongly thought through. While not every person is going to be able to follow the church through a season of church revitalization, it is unnecessary and potentially unhelpful to leave behind those who could be kept on the journey. A pastor will be unable to get everyone to agree, but a pastoral or leadership team can certainly try to allow everyone to be heard. It is important to have some plan for follow-up with those who vote against a proposed change. This could be done by asking them to not cast their vote anonymously. A leadership team would know exactly who voted for and who voted against a proposed change.

A mature leadership team would then try to address those who voted against the change to understand why. This may not go well, or it may be an immensely helpful exercise for all parties. It is possible that someone within the congregation has insight into a reason the proposed change will not work that has been missed in the formulation process. A pastor or leadership team can work diligently to see all angles but miss a part of the proposed change that needed further deliberation. Or it is possible, despite attempts at clear communication, that some within the church will misunderstand the nature of the proposed change. Churches have often been fraught with misunderstanding. The reality is that the point at which a leader is tired of talking about a vision is about the time the group starts to hear it. Sometimes people misunderstand proposed changes and need further clarification. Giving further clarification beyond the formal presentation of the change can win over some people. Some clarifications are better made in one-on-one conversation rather than in a large group. Finally, the conversation may not change the mind of the person. A congregational member may still be decidedly against the proposed change. It is still possible to ask if the congregational member would agree to disagree and not resist the change. The process of being heard may quiet dissent within the church, and mutual respect may develop for the ability to have frank, honest conversations with one another.

Strangely, it can be in the crucible of conflict that deeper intimacy with other people emerges. Conflict and disagreements managed maturely can deepen intimacy within the church, rather than cause division.[4]

It is important not to be overly idealistic about the agreeableness of people. Rarely will a church enthusiastically embrace change without any dissent. If this is happening, then it is likely those who disagree have either left the church or are not being honest about their feelings. However, if the change process is handled with wisdom and grace, it is possible to widen the group of those who are willing to give change a chance.

Pausing and Praying Together

Praying together is important. This is a key aspect of church unity in the book of Acts. I have addressed this later in the chapter by design. Prayer should permeate the church and the change process. However, prayer meetings can be used to block or drown out honest concerns and objections.

Appropriate time needs to be given to walking through an honest process of dialogue with the congregation that is punctuated with seasons of prayer. The church should not feel like praying is only used when the topic is too hot or the emotions too raw. But a change process can get out of hand if emotions become too strong. Therefore, it might be important to call for a pause in the conversation to refocus in prayer. Even so, it will be important in these moments that there is clear instruction about when the dialogue will be continued.

When praying through church direction and vision with the church, it is important to get on the same page about the nature of the prayer. Churches are often skilled at praying for individual concerns, but less skilled when it comes to praying for corporate matters. A list of prayer requests could be formulated for the change

---

4   Marcia Patton and Nora Percival, *Sacred Decisions: Consensus in Faith Communities* (Valley Forge, PA: Judson, 2021). Patton and Percival have attempted to point toward a feasible structure to move away from majority-rule models to building greater consensus. In many church settings, this approach would be more acceptable.

process. The prayer requests could include a prayer for unity, a prayer for understanding one another, a prayer for clarity of direction, a prayer for Holy Spirit consensus, a prayer for leadership, a prayer for encouragement and peace for those who disagree, and a prayer for humility and compassion for those who supported a certain change. It is only in praying from the same template that prayer will likely change the direction of the church. Sadly, prayer meetings can become occasions for promoting old positions and arguments in a purportedly spiritual tone. A poorly planned prayer time will likely not be helpful in bringing unity.

Prayer meetings are important, but they need to be used for all the church to express their need for God, for the leadership team to be willing to let go of their plans, and the congregation to contemplate embracing change that they are struggling to embrace emotionally. It should be in prayer that the church genuinely seeks only what God wants and is willing to go as slow or as fast as God desires. This type of prayer meeting can bring about profound clarity and unity, and the Holy Spirit can fall in such a way that the prayer meeting is the very place where the Holy Spirit directs and empowers his church.[5]

Leveraging Strengths

Once the history of the church is understood and the current reality of the church has been presented and analyzed, it should be easier to see the areas of strength within the church historically and in the present. While church leadership may need to do hard things in church revitalization, it would be wise to choose some areas in the visioning process that resonate with the past victories of the church and reveal how these similar victories can be achieved in the present.

Church leaders need to realize that the first series of changes will not be the last series of changes when pursuing revitalization. Church leaders rarely have the opportunity of addressing the deep-rooted issues first. The ability to garner an early win within the life of the

---

5   Richard Blackaby and Rick Foster, *Developing a Powerful Praying Church* (Jonesboro, GA: Blackaby Ministries International, 2017).

church is invaluable to being allowed to do much harder things in the future. There are situations when a challenging thing must be addressed as a first order of priority, but in many situations this is the exception, not the rule.

One way to promote church unity is to make the first series of proposed changes those that resonate with past victories as represented in the data collected from conversations within the church. This is an area where strategic action and patience will be important. There may be enthusiasm for certain changes that are good but not the most important to effecting church change. Idealistic church leadership may want to change the most important things first. However, it will be particularly important to know what the most important things for change are among most of the congregation. Even if the proposed changes do not initially address the areas the congregation considers most important, church leadership must clearly communicate that they understand the reality of these topics. Being tone-deaf to what the church wants will not win the church leadership influence in the revitalization process.

Church leadership will need to develop its approach to revitalization by seriously contemplating how this church has been able to succeed in the past and in the present. The power of contextualization gives each church a unique context in which to minister. Hopefully, churches have moved beyond the days of one-size-fits-all models for church growth. Seriously investigating how the church has been strong in the past can enable church leaders to learn new ways God may be working in this context. The best indication of what can happen in a church context is by seriously evaluating what has happened in the past. So, the easiest win within a particular context will likely be related to what has been able to happen in the past. The main exception to this rule is when the community within which the church is located has dramatically changed. If the community has dramatically changed then past successes may not be as dependable of a guide. Even in these situations, church leaders will need to point out why past strengths may not be future strengths due to the changing demographics of the mission field.

Finally, a church does not want leaders who despise their history. It is too easy to think of the current or past congregations in a negative light. The church is in decline, and those who are there have in some way contributed to this situation. The church is aware to some degree that that they are not vital. If a church leader is unable to see the bright spots in the church's history, celebrate these bright spots, and reveal how these can be repeated in the present, church leaders are unlikely to become leaders of the church. While church leaders must challenge the church beyond its current state, they cannot be dismissive of or condescending to past generations.

Managing Weaknesses

There are often deeply rooted thoughts, attitudes, and behaviors within the church community. These weaknesses can hold the church back from its full potential and will likely take years or even more than a decade to profoundly change. Making a first series of changes will not uproot generational patterns. Often the church can see the results of these generational patterns without fully realizing why they keep emerging. There is likely the need for greater self-awareness and greater understanding of the interactions within the church community to get a clearer understanding of the lack of spiritual health. These behaviors are likely also present in the family systems of many of the congregations and feel awfully familiar to the congregation, but they are often unhealthy. However, the mere realization that deeply ingrained unhealthy patterns of behavior have been present for generations is a difficult step toward spiritual health.

Church leadership needs to realize the necessity of wisdom in keeping church dysfunction at bay while trying to start the revitalization process. For example, if a church has been held back due to a complicated decision-making process that was put in place by key stakeholders within the church, then wise action will need to be developed to negotiate this. Church leaders may need to make all church discussion and decisions in full view of the congregation so key stakeholders cannot try to overturn changes. Church leaders will need to prepare themselves for old patterns to reappear. It is possible to become disillusioned when, after a series of early wins begins to propel the church toward greater revitalization, an old pattern of congregational behavior appears seemingly out of nowhere. Church leadership needs to expect that certain people within the church, often for reasons they themselves do not fully understand, will act in sinful ways, especially as a church begins to change and move forward. This is not a failure in church revitalization but part of the process of uncovering and dealing with the deep history of the church. If church leadership can maintain emotional composure in these periods and genuinely love the congregation, then they can slowly help people see old patterns of behavior that might be harming the church. This deep awareness and possibility for change among members will achieve more than mere church-revitalization goals. This level of change has the possibility of profoundly changing the lives of the congregational members. These behavior patterns are often found not just within the church but also within the personal lives of church members who are causing equal spiritual unhealth there as well.

The key to managing and striving toward healing weaknesses within the church community will require wisdom and compassion. Wisdom will both be realistic about the sinfulness of the human heart and shrewd about how to limit injurious behavior. Church leaders who believe the church community is incapable of inflicting extreme wounds will soon be hurt by the church. Those who come into the church community come for many varied reasons and motivations. Ideally, everyone would come to church for the purpose of loving God and others more. However, this ideal is not the reality. Church leaders should not be shocked by sinful behavior. They will need enough wisdom from studying the past behavior of the church to know what to look for in the present context.

Church leaders will need another necessary virtue. They must never lose compassion for those within the church. Even the church member who is extremely hard to deal with is acting this way for a reason. There is likely a rationale for their behavior that, if fully understood, would not justify the behavior but would certainly explain it more clearly. If church leadership could truly know all that has led church members to be deceitful, angry, vindictive, or noncommittal, then likely church leaders would be far more compassionate toward them. Church leaders must be able to see the struggle of the individual church members and never forget that central to the mission of the church is learning to love and encourage growth among those who are there.

WRITING THE NEXT CHAPTER OF THE CHURCH

A particular church's history is a reliable guide into what it will allow. If church leaders can accurately read the history of a church and listen carefully in the present, they will be able to discern what is possible within this church. While it is important to analyze the community where the church is located, knowing the church itself is especially important because it will be through the vehicle of the people of the church that the community will be reached. If a church leader does not know the people who make up the church, it will be difficult to mobilize them to reach a community. Church leaders must speak the language not only of the community but also of the church.

It is often good to start with the end in mind. Imagine that the time of ministry is over at a particular church. For example, if the current church leadership could be effective for ten years, how would the story be written? It is important to carefully think through what earlier pastors and church leaders experienced, what successes they had, and what seems doable in this season of the church.

It may be particularly important to write this prospective chapter of the church. This chapter can then imaginatively be placed next to the other chapters of the church. Even though it has not been lived out, does it fit? Would it be viewed by the current church as a bright chapter? What would be the most memorable event of this chapter? If a pastor can play this chapter out in his mind and it resonates, then he is likely onto a real plan. If a pastor or church leaders can design the story of the church with this prospective chapter, it would be remarkably interesting to hear the responses from the congregation. If there is disbelief among those in the church that what they've written

could happen, then earlier chapters of church history could be refer-
enced to show that it is possible because it has happened in the past. It
will be important to practice this narrative. Being able to tell a future
story of the church will be more compelling than just recommending
changes. The necessary changes of church revitalization will need to
be connected to a compelling narrative that will not only instruct
the church on what to do but also give the church a vision of what it
can be. The beautiful thing about telling a future story while living
in a bright chapter of a church's history is that the painful periods of
the past recede into the background and the general sense about the
church becomes positive.

CHAPTER 4

DEEPER THAN DEMOGRAPHICS

A church exists in a community. There is a sense that every church is influenced and appropriated to the culture around it. God has created a world in which various cultures and languages are present. Rather than being intimidated by the vastness of the cultures of the world, there is a sense that the Christian should embrace the beauty evidenced in the diversity of the world. The beauty of a church in various cultural contexts that has both appropriated and translated the beauty of the gospel through the forms of a unique culture is a wonderful sight to see. Sometimes the changing cultural landscape can cause a pastor to fail to see the beauty of the community in which he serves. It is important for a pastor to step back for a moment, to gaze at his community, and to ponder how the beauty of God's design is evidenced through the expressions of those made in the image of God in his community.[1]

---

1   Michael Wagenman, *Engaging the World with Abraham Kuyper* (Bellingham, WA: Lexham, 2019). Abraham Kuyper sets forth a plan for engaging society that is worthy of imitation at many points.

UNDERSTANDING THE
SECULARIZING MOMENT

A major factor in the need for church revitalization is the decline of the Judeo-Christian ethos that used to pervade the American landscape. The impulse for the average American, especially in the American South, was toward participation in a church. Many of the great churches of America were able to capitalize on this American moment to build large buildings in their communities. Churches were more than a solely religious community during this era of American history. Churches aided in establishing the social order, making good citizens, and providing community fellowship along with accomplishing a religious function. What seems to be in steepest decline in America is the civic Christian culture pervasive in past decades. There is a mixed report on the actual loss of genuine Christian commitment.[2]

The decline in the Judeo-Christian ethos has been coupled with the decline of the American community. The power of social media and globalization has put the world at our fingertips but seemed to have distanced many from genuine community. Many people do not know their neighbors, or they live in such a heavily populated area that there are too many neighbors to know. It is less common for Americans to be part of social groups than in previous times. Social capital is the value of social networks and relationships that enables communities to thrive. The power of connection is especially important to the overall health of a person and of society.[3] Churches have historically been places where community can thrive and need to lean into this cultural moment and offer the connection that many in the community desperately need.

The mood toward church life has diminished. American culture is moving into a post-Christian era. The place of the church in this

---

2   Roger Finke and Rodney Stark, *The Churching of America, 1776–2005: Winners and Losers in Our Religious Economy* (New Brunswick, NJ: Rutgers University Press, 2005). Finke and Stark argue that America has greater religious participation now than in the past.
3   Robert Putnam, *Bowling Alone: The Collapse and Revival of American Community* (New York: Simon & Schuster, 2000).

unfamiliar environment will be different than in past generations. Church participation is no longer the default setting of most American adults. Churches are feeling the strain of being one of many options, even in smaller communities. The lack of social pressure to attend church has dropped. Therefore, churches cannot assume that new families moving into the community will look for a church. Churches must be willing to offer ministries, programs, and community projects that engage and invite those within the community into the church community.

Further, the mindset of many within the American community is changing. While mainline denominations have declined along with the broader world of evangelicalism, those identifying as religiously unaffiliated are becoming more prevalent. The rise of the religiously unaffiliated (or the nones) also affects the need for the church to contextualize.[4] This is especially difficult for ministers who lived in an American context that was more influenced by a Judeo-Christian worldview. Presuppositions that are necessary for robust belief are held in suspicion or uncertainty by a sizeable portion of the population. The simple beliefs of the existence of God, the reality of human sin, and the need for salvation that in previous generations were the place that conversations began can no longer be assumed as a foundational belief among those within the community. This has hindered older models of evangelism that assumed a large number of Christian beliefs held by the public.

The current moment is pervaded with a spirit of anti-institutionalism. Along with this spirit is a declining respect for clergy. This does not mean that hope is lost, but clergy must demonstrate their credibility in and benefit for the community. These things can no longer be assumed. While one can demur the decline in clergy respect, this is not a feature that is unique to clergy. The current cultural mood seems to be that many leaders have failed them so community leaders must show their competence before they are trusted.[5] A pastor who

---

4   Ryan Burge, *The Nones: Where They Came From, Who They Are, Where They Are Going* (Minneapolis: Fortress, 2021), 95–122. Burge reveals that many of the nones do not fit the standard atheist/agnostic profile of a past era.
5   David Kinnaman and Gabe Lyons, *Good Faith: Being a Christian When Society Thinks You're Irrelevant and Extreme* (Grand Rapids: Baker Books,

is willing to serve his community should be able to overcome this skepticism through simple acts of clarity and steadfastness throughout many years.

A more difficult hurdle for pastors to overcome is the lack of church commitment among many. The dominant mood is that spirituality can and even should be practiced outside institutional religion. Simply, many do not understand the function that a church could and should play in their spiritual lives. Here again is an opportunity to avoid defensiveness and rather to lean into the moment with clarity. First, a person's spirituality is often viewed through the lens of individualism.[6] Americans customarily look within themselves to attempt to discern the answers to their problems. Christianity points to a need for individuals to look outside themselves to God, who is ready to provide answers to humanity's plight. Further, while the role of the individual is important within Christianity, the power of community is highlighted. The idea that a person can mature spirituality apart from community is foreign to our faith. God has provided the gifts of the church to build up the church and enable the maturity of believers. The church needs to show the power of community in shaping one's spiritual life and the need to look outside ourselves to God, who stands ready to provide for us.[7] Second, churches can respond to the idea that self-discovered spirituality is a superior path to ancient paths of spirituality. The institutional church can point to practices in its history that it has found to be both helpful and harmful. The concept that self-directed spiritual pursuits will be more beneficial rather than taking the best from ancient practices seems to be on its face false. A compelling case can be made that self-directed spirituality without the guides of ancient practices has far more potential

---

2017), 11–66. Kinnaman and Lyons reveal the changing place of Christianity within wider American culture and provide recommendations for adjusting to these realities.

6   Carl Truman, *The Rise and Triumph of the Modern Self: Cultural Amnesia Expressive Individualism, and the Road to Sexual Revolution* (Wheaton, IL: Crossway, 2020), 35–104.

7   Charles Taylor, *A Secular Age* (Cambridge: MA: Belknap, 2007), 423–778.

for harm than institutional religion.[8] The church should position itself in a culture like a guide rather than an expert in these ancient Christian practices. The presence of aberrant religious ideas and practices has potential to bring about more spiritual harm than wisely run institutional Christianity. The church can reawaken the culture to the best of the past while avoiding mistakes the institutional church has made.

MISSIONARY MINDSET IN YOUR COMMUNITY

A pastor should not think that because he is familiar with a community that he understands the majority of those who reside there. He must learn to observe his community through fresh eyes and understand people around him with a deeper insight. The community life of individuals radically shapes their identity. In many ways, what a community promotes and participates in reveals a great deal about what motivates a person or community. The idea that we are what we love is a very insightful concept.[9]

A pastor observes his community for specific reasons. His goal is to encourage his community to become authentic worshipers of Jesus. The church needs revitalization because of a spiritual problem. The object of devotion of those both within and outside the church is not focused on worshiping God and working for his kingdom. But understanding what has gone wrong requires discernment. Sin is anything that removes God from his place. It is closely related to the concept of idolatry. That which takes God's place in a person's life is not necessarily bad but has been exalted to a status that only God should possess.

This subtle drift toward putting things in the place that only God should have can happen easily in a person's life. While one may assume that our thinking is the window to our soul, it may be that our objects of love are a far better indication of our devotion. The

---

8   Ross Douthat, *Bad Religion: How We Became a Nation of Heretics* (New York: Simon & Schuster, 2012).

9   James K. A. Smith, *Desiring the Kingdom: Worship, Worldview, and Cultural Formation* (Grand Rapids: Baker Academic, 2009).

simple question "What do you want?" can provide real insight into core values and loves of a person. A pastor can and should use this framework to think more deeply about his community.

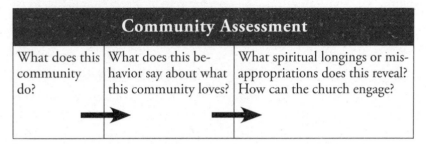

Community Assessment		
What does this community do?	What does this behavior say about what this community loves?	What spiritual longings or mis-appropriations does this reveal? How can the church engage?

While the question of loves can be used on an individual level, it can also be used on a community level. A pastor can step back and ask the question, "What does this community love?" The answer to this question is not deep or philosophical. American communities love economic growth, football, community festivals, tourism, recreation space, and so forth. The priorities of a community become obvious when stepping back and looking at the community. A pastor then needs to ask the question, "Why does this community have these loves?" Reflecting at this level can give real insight into the devotion of a community. The community has devoted itself to focusing on these goals with the intention of seeing some end achieved. Strangely, many give themselves to objectives without a clear-eyed vision as to why these objectives are being pursued. Many disheartened pastors have watched as church members have made church life less and less of a priority, while giving themselves with great devotion and passion to other causes. A pastor and the church leadership need to be able to step back for a moment and ask why this is the case. Church leadership should be willing to have eyes of discernment and compassion at this moment.

Church leaders should not think that most church members and attendees fully understand why they are devoting themselves to these patterns of life. Our loves are obvious in what we do. It is hard to hide our loves because that which we love we give ourselves to. Sadly, humans are known for loving the wrong things, giving ourselves to poor loves that will not supply what we desire. Further, that which we do further shapes and refines our character and our loves. So, church leaders may need to slowly, graciously understand what the community loves, why they love these things, and what the outcome is from loving these things. At this precise point, church leaders may be able to understand the worship life of a person with greater clarity than the person understands himself or herself. Just like a doctor understands the human body better than the patient, or the therapist understands emotional states better than the client, church leaders can be able to understand the shape of a person's or a community's devotion with greater clarity than they themselves do.[10]

To start the process of discernment, church leaders will need to answer the following questions: What does this community do? How do the activities of this community inform what they love? What does the community hope to achieve in giving itself to these loves? What leaders will often discover is that the actions many communities perform are not inherently bad, but these activities may have taken a place that only God should have. Therefore, there will be some benefit from these actions, but they will be unsatisfactory for the human heart. A person will not find rest until they find rest in God and earnest, heartfelt devotion toward God. Therefore, a pastor may not need to state that everything a community is doing is inherently wrong, but that many good things have received an overly exalted place that only God should have.

For example, many church-revitalization situations in the United States are found in rural contexts. There is often a powerful sense of nostalgia in these communities, a deep love for a previous era. This keen sense of nostalgia holds on a community level, not just at a church level. Pastors and church leaders are often frustrated that the church wants not to move forward into the future but to retreat into the past. It is easy for pastors and church leaders to be dismissive of

---

10   James K. A. Smith, *You Are What You Love: The Spiritual Power of Habit* (Grand Rapids: Brazos, 2016), 1–56.

persons who think like this, but leaders may need to think more deeply. Church leaders can simply apply many of the questions previously set forth. What does the church member do? The answer attempts to move the church into a past era. What does the church member love? The answer is a sense of familiarity, comfort, and worship that was discovered in a previous era. What does the church member believe he or she will achieve by going back to this previous era? The answer is whatever he or she feels was lost from that era. Further, a church member like this in many rural communities has lost some level of hope for the future. In many rural communities, the effects of globalization have affected many areas of the community for the worse. There is not just a sense that a past era was better for the church, but in the minds of many that past era was better for the community. So, deep down the desire to retreat to a past era is well-intentioned based on the desired outcomes a person believes it will bring about. However, often these church members' focus is so enthusiastic about reclaiming a past era that their love blinds them to present realities. A pastor will potentially need to affirm the beauty and benefits of a past era, grieve with them that some particularly good things are gone, and redirect them to the present moment where God is still active in both similar and diverse ways. Church leaders will need to direct the love of church members to loving what God is doing and can do in the present, rather than futilely attempting to reclaim a past era. A person in their fifties can never be twenty again but can celebrate the memories of being twenty and live well in the moment at fifty with similar but different joys. A gracious pastor will help a church member let go of past fantasies and live in the reality of God's presence in the here and now.

Another example is that many American families have both parents working full-time jobs with their children in many extracurricular activities. Again, a pastor or church leaders can observe this situation and ask the same series of questions. What do these families do? The parents are working a lot and the children are remarkably busy. What do they love? Likely, the parents are giving themselves to achieving a certain financial status or giving themselves to jobs for the fortification of identity. The children are giving themselves to education and extracurricular programs. What is this family attempting to achieve by following this path? There is often the objective that a certain financial status, quality education, and extracurricular activities will lead to the good life for the family. Sadly, many American families are tired, disconnected, and hurried. Again, having adequate money, quality education, and extracurricular activities are not inherently bad, but if these get positioned as an object of devotion that will provide the good life then disappointment will be the outcome. A pastor will need to graciously reveal to many families in their community that the good life they are pursuing is not realized and that a different approach is needed. Helping families see that their current loves may not be loving them back well can graciously redirect them to put God back in his rightful place and order these other good things within their right, but limited, place in a person's life.

To be able to develop this level of discernment, church leaders will need to analyze their own loves as well. Church leaders may love church revitalization or church success as a misplaced love. If a pastor is constantly giving himself to church work, then he must ask himself why. If the answers are to encourage people to be in right relationship with God and to see the beauty of the church emerge, then he has that opportunity every day in varying degrees. However, a pastor can easily slip into loving church success to fortify his identity, salve feelings for importance, and more. A pastor who is diligently placing God in his rightful place will know the struggle of this process and will be able to graciously guide others around him.

GENERATIONAL AWARENESS

A pastor ministers to people who live in different realities because of the various events that have shaped their lives. There are not just characteristics of communities in which people live, but characteristics of eras in which people were born. People who lived together through certain events have a different outlook and priorities because of the events that shaped important eras of their life. A younger pastor will have to work with older generations, and older pastors will need to relate to younger generations. The vision of intergenerational church communities is growing rarer. Many churches are primarily one demographic stratum. This is not a plan for revitalization. Therefore, generational awareness is necessary to reach new people from various generations.

There are four major generations present in the contemporary church: baby boomers, Gen X, millennials, and Gen Z. The baby boomers are currently the oldest major generation in churches. Because of its size, this generation has had an enormous influence on church and society, virtually overshadowing Gen X. The formative years of the 1960s and 1970s changed the landscape of America. The boomers were influenced by the end of World War II, the civil rights movement, and the war in Vietnam.

Gen X was shaped by a new America of rising divorce rates, more women in the workforce, the AIDS epidemic, and the first generation to have personal computers. This group often is the forgotten child among the current generations.[11]

The millennial generation was the first generation to fully experience the internet age. The 9/11 attacks marked this generation, and they learned to live in an age of terror. The great recession made some millennials less optimistic about their financial future. Because their lives are so digitally connected, millennials value authenticity, community, and stability.[12]

Gen Z is currently rising. The value of technology, a more pluralistic and diverse outlook on life, and deeper questions about sexuality are current realities of this generation.[13] Church leadership needs to realize that while people live in the same community, the life events, outlooks, and priorities of various generations can be vastly different.

---

11   Elisabeth Nesbit Sbanotto and Craig Blomberg, *Effective Generational Ministry: Biblical and Practical Insights for Transforming Church Communities* (Grand Rapids: Baker Academic, 2016), 1–166.

12   Barna Group, *Making Space for Millennials: A Blueprint for Your Culture, Ministry, Leadership and Facilities* (Ventura, CA: Barna Group, 2014).

13   Barna Group, *Gen Z: The Culture, Beliefs and Motivations Shaping the Next Generation* (Ventura, CA: Barna Group, 2018).

A healthy, vitalized church attempts to make peace among generations and establish meaningful, intergenerational conversations and learning.

THE DIVIDED STATES OF AMERICA

A church should influence the wider culture around it. How the church engages the culture especially the political environment will differ among Christians. Many church members see very little difference between their political and their religious views, while others see them as separate. For many, it is the worldview provided to them by Christianity that enables them to make ethical judgments on a variety of issues. It is certainly true that political decisions are often related to one's moral outlook. Christians need balance and thoughtfulness when thinking about how to address political turmoil that does not seem to abate. A pastor can be pulled into the conversation regarding Christianity and politics. Thoughtful cultural engagement can help, but unreflective engagement may be an obstacle to church revitalization.

There are several justifiable ways for a Christian to engage the political moment. One's approach to the church and politics is related to one's vision of culture and the church's witness to the wider world. First, a pastor can understand the church and the culture as separate. This pastor has written off culture as a place from which the church needs to distance itself; one must find solace in the believing community. According to this view, Christ is against culture and the church must carve out its existence within a hostile space. It is certainly true that Christians are to live out their identity as strangers and aliens in a foreign world. The church stands in opposition to the world and operates a kingdom that lives by certain principles that are foreign to the kingdoms of the world. The kingdom of God is an upside-down kingdom. The idea that the church and culture are separate can be required to correct the desire to conform to the contemporary morality of the world. The negative side of this approach is that the church can become too isolated and lose its missionary spirit. Culture can perceive the church as an institution that is isolated from the world versus a community sent into the world to be salt and light.

Second, a pastor could believe that the church and politics operate in God's world but do so in different spheres. For example, while the church is to be a community that welcomes all and is ready to forgive, the government stands ready to execute justice on those who bring disorder to society. These are two vastly contrasting functions, but they cooperate to fulfill God's plan. The church is to live out its mission and the government is to live out its purposes, and even though these functions are vastly different they operate according to a larger divine plan. It is equally true to say that God uniquely uses his church to bring about his purposes in the world but is still working through all the affairs of humanity to bring the world to an appropriate end. This approach certainly realizes the distinct function of the church and the government. It can appreciate their unique roles and articulate what is and what is not the role of the church in the world. This approach, however, can limit cultural interaction because the function of the church in the world operates in a different realm than government.

Third, a pastor could understand the church as having a prophetic role to the culture. Many different church communities have taken on the prophetic role to varying degrees. It is often raised by a minority group that is pointing out oppression and injustice in the wider culture—for example, historically black churches during the era of Jim Crow. But it has also been utilized in historically white churches. With the cultural shift to a less white, less Protestant America and with the legal acceptance of moral issues that are outside historic Christianity, the prophetic voice has been raised to recapture aspects of a previous era. These prophetic voices are moving in two different directions. In historically black churches, the prophetic voice continues to set forth a vision of equality that still needs to be achieved. In many historically white churches, the prophetic voice is still setting forth aspects of an era that need to be recaptured. These competing prophetic voices can clearly be at odds with one another. It would take a skilled pastor to show that in one sense the Christian church in America needs to achieve certain moral standards that it has not achieved, while also pointing out that there are aspects of a previous era that need to be recaptured. This dialogue is full of conflict and highly emotional. As a pastor enters this dialogue, clarity of purpose and message will need to be considered to avoid misunderstanding.

The prophetic voice has been positive throughout history. Without courageous pastors who are willing to take a moral stand, social change would be unlikely. However, the manner of social change is seen as top-down in this approach. The prophetic voice is typically seeking large-scale social change through changes in laws. This requires a close working relationship between pastors who seek change and politicians who can push legislation. This process, albeit necessary to effect the type of change that is being sought, comes with many obstacles. A pastor can quickly become compromised in such a political environment or give the appearance of compromise. Many pastors will attempt to communicate the necessity of compromise when operating in this sphere by appealing to the lesser evil. However, this creates a negative perception among some churchgoers who would prefer their pastor stay out of the fray. On the other hand, a pastor who is willing to enter this fray can also gain a large following. Yet the message of the gospel is interlaced with tactics for governmental reform. In the worst-case scenario, the ultimate belief in the transformative power of the gospel in the hearts of people can be replaced by the necessity of right legislation that will lead to a more Christian America.[14] There are clear points to make on all sides. A nation that has immoral laws will be influenced toward greater immorality. However, right laws will not change the heart of humanity, and the continual slide away from Judeo-Christian values reveals that even with the push of prophetic movements on all sides and the sinfulness of the human heart, radical transformation is still greatly needed.

Fourth, a pastor can take a more local, incremental approach to the transformation of culture. The prophetic-voice tradition primarily seeks top-down change, whereas a transformative approach seeks bottom-up, inside-out transformation. Working within the context of

---

14   Andrew Whitehead and Samuel Perry, *Taking America Back for God: Christian Nationalism in the United States* (Oxford: Oxford University Press, 2020), 23–53.

a missional church to seek transformation of its members along with the transformation of the culture around it is the primary objective. A transformative approach first takes very seriously the transformation of those within the church. Merely being a Christian does not mean that one's life is transformed into the thoughts, feelings, and behaviors of Jesus. Christianity places intentionality on formation within the community of faith. Jesus sends transformed Christians to missionally enter the community. While the gospel is uttermost, the Christian community seeks to bring goodness to all aspects of community life. Ideally, Christians should hold social good and gospel proclamation in close connection without the neglect of either. This approach is slower and does not promise as much as the top-down prophetic approach. Whereas the top-down prophetic approach can get a clear win through the overturning of a law or the passage of a piece of legislation, the transformative approach is slower and more incremental but potentially affects more change for the recipients of it than a top-down approach. This is a worthy method and creates good in the community where the church resides. It will still likely be criticized by some who state it does not do enough, fast enough, to stem the tide of secularism. Theoretically, however, if all evangelical churches were to take this approach for a consistent period, then cultural transformation would occur due to transformed hearts not mere legal pronouncement. The tension remains, as the ultimate goal for the Christian church is not to attempt to outlaw certain behaviors so that people cannot do them but to see people's hearts change to such a degree that they desire to not do them.[15]

In the social media age, the political discourse even among Christians has reached a fever pitch. Many of the arguments on social media are not rooted in clear thinking and Christian love but in heated emotional rhetoric. The current approach in our increasingly digital public square is not helping bring about wholeness and reconciliation.

---

15 Amy Black, ed., *Five Views on the Church and Politics* (Grand Rapids: Zondervan, 2015), and D. A. Carson, *Christ and Culture Revisited* (Grand Rapids: Eerdmans, 2008), 1–66.

The role of emotion and the holding of certain virtues and worldviews affects the way a person makes religious and political decisions. An attempt to understand the deep world of emotion in rationality and the attempt to understand the axiomatic truths underneath the political rhetoric may not bring greater agreement initially but may bring about greater understanding.[16] This seems like a welcome next step.

A necessity for all Christians whatever their approach to culture and politics is to remember the character qualities of Christian communication and behavior. There is never a time to be ungodly, and there is never a time to speak of others in a non-Christian way. The commands of Jesus that call us to love our enemies (Matt. 5:44) cannot justify name-calling and blatantly disrespectful speech or actions toward others.

Last, a pastor who is attempting to pursue church revitalization will not have ample time to get into the fray of every political issue when the very existence of a local church is in jeopardy. A pastor will by necessity need to think about the care of the congregation, casting a vision for the church, and working diligently to see basic actions accomplished to move the church into a place of greater stability. A pastor attempting to change the world, before attending to the immediate needs of a dying church, may end up with a dead church and an increasingly secular world. There is a sense in church revitalization that if a pastor cannot convince a small band of Christians to live into the ideals of Christianity to make a church flourish, there is little chance the church will have the ability to address greater cultural ills. Many churches that decry the secularization of America fail to make even the smallest changes within their church to reach out to the next generation.

GLOBALIZATION AND THE NEED FOR CULTURAL INTELLIGENCE

The forces of globalization and digitization have made the world both larger and smaller. A pastor no longer must be evaluated only against

---

16 Jonathan Haidt, *The Righteous Mind: Why Good People Are Divided by Politics and Religion* (New York: Vintage, 2012).

the pastor down the street but against every pastor in America that is on social media. Further, church members can encounter every version of religious teaching at their fingertips. A rural church no longer has the luxury of living separated from the vastness of the world. A pastor should not feel overwhelmed by this. Every person attending a church is encountering this level of information overload. A pastor should not attempt to be an expert on the complexity of the world that is around him but should be an example of a thoughtful, prayerful, humble learner amid the complexity of not only local problems but also global ones. No one can be an expert or even process through the amount of information poured out daily.

While a pastor and church leaders should not feel the responsibility to understand all the effects of globalization, he should have a general awareness of it. Cultural intelligence relates to the ability of a person to understand and relate to various trends and cultures. A pastor must realize that even within traditional American communities there is a vastness in how individuals think and live. Rather than attempting to be a cultural expert, a pastor must learn to be a cultural learner. Some pastors think that learning and integrating responsibly into the culture compromises the gospel message. A change in method, however, does not mean a change in message. Christian missionaries have utilized cultural intelligence for years as they have attempted gospel communication in international contexts. With the reality of globalization, the same missionary techniques that were used in international contexts must now be used in the American context. The world has come to America, and America to the world. Therefore, the strict separation of ideas, customs, and practices are not contained geographically but are contained among groups that share similar ideas. Within one American community, there are many subcommunities that are quite different from one another even though they live near one another.[17] Further, since people can personalize community through ease of travel and digital means, the need to

---

17 Darrell Bock, *Cultural Intelligence: Living for God in a Diverse, Pluralistic World* (Nashville: B&H Academic, 2020), 85–128.

connect and create a homogeneous culture with those in proximity is no longer a necessity.

Just because a pastor knows a person's age, race, gender, and community location does not mean that the pastor understands the person. Cultural intelligence will seek to understand each person, express empathy, push away bias, listen closely, and observe carefully how they live. A pastor must develop cultural intelligence and a missionary outlook even in a community that he believes he understands. The moment a pastor stops learning the community around him will be the moment he starts misunderstanding the community and overlooking many of those he is attempting to reach.

READING A DEMOGRAPHIC STUDY

A demographic study is a great tool to help a pastor understand the community around him and can give community data about a church.[18] For example, a pastor ought to know how many people are within a ten-mile radius and what the profile of these people is. A general rule of thumb is that people are willing to drive ten miles to attend a church. This can vary depending on whether an area is heavily or sparsely populated. If the people within this radius are the ones a church is most likely to reach, it is important to know how many there are and who they are.

As another general rule of thumb, an extremely healthy church can reach about 5 percent of those within a ten-mile radius as an average attendance on Sunday morning. For example, if a church has twenty-thousand people in a ten-mile radius, then an extremely healthy church would have around one thousand people in attendance. This should be set as a goal for how many people it is reasonable for a church to reach.

Further, it is important to know the breakdown of the demographics of the area. For example, what is the average age within the communi-

---

18 Demographic studies can be purchased for one's community from many sources. However, one source to purchase a demographic study is www. churchanswers.com.

ty? Does the area trend younger or older? Is there a sizable percentage of families with children or not? Are there a lot of singles in the area? What is the average income? Are families affluent, or are they struggling financially? What is the breakdown of races? Is there a majority race in the area, or is the area more diverse? Do people in this region share similar beliefs due to their location in this community? These are questions that can be answered factually. A demographic study can give hard data on a series of questions. If a pastor is going to faithfully reach his community, he must know the data on those he is trying to reach.

The shape of the community will affect the best type of ministry to offer. If the area is aging, then it will likely be unwise to create a worship-service experience for a younger audience. If there is a large group of singles, then it would be unwise to gear all the church programming toward those who are married. If the area is affluent, then it is likely that a mercy ministry will be less needed than in places where there are lower incomes and greater need. A pastor and his leadership must learn to see and accept the community that is around him and learn to minister to it. A key mistake in church revitalization is learning to minister to the church and the people that are in the church without a wider perspective of the community. Many American communities have changed radically, which is one of the main reasons that a church model that worked for so many years no longer works. A pastor may need to carefully read a demographic study and seriously ask himself the question as to whether he is suited and desires to minister to this community. If a pastor wants to minister to a young, trendy congregation and he is situated in an area that is aging and traditional in its mindset, one may need to contemplate whether this is the place of ministry for him. It is better on the front end to be honest with oneself about communities in which one can minister and in which communities one cannot. It will do great damage to the church and likely to a pastor if there is a mismatch of personality and styles. A demographic study gives a pastor hard data on the type of people he will need to reach. If he feels like he does not want to or cannot reach people of this profile, then he should step back from this revitalization effort.

LISTENING TO YOUR COMMUNITY

Some pastors, however, are so interested in reading demographic reports and making plans in isolation that they fail to interact with the very community they are trying to reach. A demographic report can take on new light as a pastor talks and interacts with those in the community. Church leaders can and should implement this in simple ways. In many communities there are places where the community meets to interact. This could be at a local restaurant, a sporting event, a community festival, or during a community meeting. A pastor should not be absent in these moments.

If a pastor desires those within the community to become invested in the church, it will be important that the pastor invests in the community. A great deal of learning can occur just by hanging out with the community. A pastor can, if appropriate, ask those in the community about what type of church they would attend. It is important that a pastor not simply hope the community shares his vision for church life but that he is open to what they have to say. There are many reasons people do not attend church. Simply being able to identify obstacles to church attendance and remove them will be important in the revitalization effort. Further, a pastor will get a much better idea of what will be tolerable to those in his community regarding a church experience by listening carefully to those within the community.

DISCERNING A CULTURALLY APPROPRIATE APPROACH

The beauty of the church is evident in its diversity. There is still a place for many distinct types of cultural expressions of church life. For a church to revitalize, the form of church that is attempted must be in line with the people of the church and the community. A pastor must be able to develop a culturally appropriate approach to revitalization that is able to answer the following four questions.

First, is this approach to church revitalization in line with the current members of the church? There is often a disconnect between the church members and the community at large. However, it will take more than a pastor desiring to reach the community. The church will need to see the vision for those within the community who are reachable. It may take time for a pastor to be able to show the congregation the reality of those who need to be reached within the community. If a pastor attempts to reach those people without the support of the church, there will likely be a great deal of frustration when someone from the community attends the church only to receive a poor reception. The church must be jointly ready to welcome a certain group within the community. Merely going out and starting to bring people to the church without adequate buy-in will frustrate the leadership and will not reach those who attempt to integrate within the fellowship.

Second, is this approach to church revitalization in line with the demographics of the community? A church must reach who is already in the community, not solely who they wish to be in the community. If the community has a large group of single mothers, then the church will need to mobilize a church structure that is conducive to this reality. Many churches have the ideal member they may want to have as part of their fellowship. However, this ideal of a young middle-class family with children is becoming an increasingly smaller portion of the American populace. A church cannot assume that a church will revitalize by reaching young families with children. This simply may not be the dominant demographic in the community.

Third, is this approach to church revitalization suitable to the personality and talents of the pastoral staff? Once a pastor and the staff can clearly see the mission field that is around them, they need to step back and ask whether they have the skill set to reach these people. While God can certainly use anyone to reach people, there are certain types of people who are better able to reach certain groups. A pastor may need to carefully think through who he hires on the pastoral staff that would enable him to shape the staff in accordance with the needs of the area. A pastor must carefully understand the type of person he must be and the type of staff he must develop to be able to reach the community around him.

Fourth, is the approach to church revitalization expansive enough to enable the church to reach a critical mass sufficient for revitalization to occur? A church cannot reach everyone. However, a church must reach some of the people around them. If a church is attempting to reach a group within the community, they must ask the simple question of whether there are enough people within reach of the church to achieve a critical mass. It is always possible to attempt to reach a large subsection of the population. While it is ideal and noble to attempt to be a church for everyone and a church should strive for this ideal as much as possible, the church will primarily reach a certain group or groups of people. If a church is attempting to achieve revitalization, then it must be able to reach a sizable portion of this group.

CHAPTER 5

EVALUATING THE PASTORAL PROFILE AND PERSONAL WELLNESS PLAN

A pastor should not underestimate the personal toll that will occur by leading a church through revitalization. Often, pastors are not able to see the process of church revitalization to completion because of their own emotional and spiritual fatigue. The process of church revitalization should be measured in years, not months. Therefore, maintaining stamina for several months or even a few years will not be sufficient to see the process completed. A pastor must take the perspective of a marathon runner, not a sprinter. He must learn to be faithful to accomplish the necessary tasks to keep the church moving forward without becoming overly depleted personally. This chapter attempts to combine two elements of evaluation into one. A pastor can become extremely focused on becoming a better leader through understanding his personality and leadership style. This is an important task a pastor should complete. However, this same pastor may not pay careful attention to his own personal wellness. In the midst, of leading well a pastor may not be living well. This chapter thus attempts to balance the ability of a pastor to lead well while also living well. Spiritual maturity and resiliency should grow as a pastor's spiritual life grows. Ideally, pastors increase in resiliency over time as they mature. The difficulty of loving people who are constant obstacles to church revitalization should become easier as maturity is attained. Nevertheless, some pastors struggle under the stress of ministry. This chapter appeals to these pastors to understand the spiritual resources available to them in Christ and to grow in resiliency and maturity. A pastor who is so focused on being a high-functioning leader needs to make sure there is sufficient transparency and vulnerability about where he is in his personal life.

BIBLICAL REQUIREMENT FOR PASTORAL LEADERSHIP

Much preparation for ministry is concentrated on theological learning and practical ministry skills. These are necessary areas of competency, but they may overlook the central biblical requirements for pastoral ministry, which are associated with character (1 Tim. 3:1–7). The need for strong character and a pastoral temperament is given primacy in the biblical text.[1] The need for gentleness, self-control, and generosity are rooted in strong character. Therefore, a pastor should not overlook the need for personal integrity and character as essential requirements for pastoral ministry. A pastor must have a strong grasp of areas in which his character is well-developed and areas that he is vulnerable to sinful behaviors. Developing character is not a secondary issue in pastoral readiness but an essential qualification for pastoral ministry.

WRITING YOUR OWN HISTORY

There are few tools better to help a pastor understand himself than writing out a history. It is best to write two different histories, a personal history and a pastoral history. A pastor writes a personal history to track

---

1   Philip Towner, *The Letters to Timothy and Titus*, New International Commentary on the New Testament (Grand Rapids: Eerdmans, 2006), 247–59.

his spiritual progress over time. A pastor writes his pastoral history to understand the trajectory of his own pastorates. It is unwise to avoid reflection on seasons of life and the shape of previous pastorates.

A personal history focuses on your spiritual progress over time. This history can start preconversion to talk about the factors that led to faith in Christ. After conversion, there should be an honest assessment about seasons of growth and seasons of stagnation and decline. A pastor should be very aware about the factors that led him to faith in Christ. It could have been the influence of godly parents, a faithful pastor, a friend, or an experience. A pastor's spiritual journey certainly will affect the way he ministers and thinks about ministry. A pastor should know in which season of his life he grew the most. If a pastor is unaware of the conditions under which he grows the most, how is he to make sure that he stays in these conditions? For example, a pastor may have grown in spiritual maturity while in a small group of peers in seminary. It will be important for that pastor to make sure that he is able to find a group of peers while pastoring to study the Bible and share about his life. A failure to do this may cause a pastor's spiritual life to dry up. A pastor needs to be honest about his sin, especially his habitual sin. Every person has areas in their life in which they struggle. A pastor setting out to lead a church through revitalization will face challenges in these very areas. Leading church revitalization is an incredibly stressful endeavor, and challenges to areas of vulnerability will arise. It is important for a pastor to not only be aware of old sin patterns but also to develop a comprehensive plan to address these sin patterns when they emerge. A pastor can best develop a comprehensive plan to address sin patterns in community with others who are mature and confidential. A pastor (or any Christian) is unlikely to have victory over a difficult sin pattern without the help of the Christian community. Moral failure in the pastorate harms a pastor, his family, the church family, and the wider witness of the church. It is incredibly sad when a successful pastor can work through the difficulties of pastoring a church but is unable to win over sin in his own life.

The history of a pastor's pastorates is different from his own personal history. In a personal history, a pastor documents the various seasons in his life that primarily address learning about the pastor's personal spiritual health. The history of pastorates is understanding the dynamics of past ministry. A pastor should be able to articulate what he liked and what he disliked about his pastorates. If the pastor is young and has limited pastoral experience, then he should evaluate all previous ministry experience. A pastor will not find the same level of enjoyment and fulfillment in every ministry setting and should not set himself up for failure by being unaware of the ministry contexts in which he flourishes and in which he struggles. If a pastor has multiple pastorates, there are typically patterns that occur of which the pastor is unaware. If a pastor has a pattern of staying in a pastorate five years or fewer and then moving on, this is a clue that the pastor tends to move on to other churches rather than addressing a deeper personal or leadership issue. A pastor can complete both a personal and pastoral history on a whiteboard or a sheet of paper. The initial goal would be to merely document major moments in a pastor's personal and pastoral life. Then these major events would need further description and contextualization. Last, larger analysis needs to occur, such as: In what moments did the pastor grow or decline in his spiritual life? What were the causes? What patterns emerge? For example, what is the average tenure? What are the typical conflicts? What false expectations are set at the beginning of the pastorate? How did the relationship with the church end? These questions can point to areas of deep self-awareness.[2]

UNDERSTANDING PERSONALITY TESTS

Many pastors utilize personality tests to help them discover their strengths and weaknesses in leadership. While they can certainly be a useful tool in the process of self-analysis, in the life of the church an honest team of elders that can speak into the life of a pastor will typically be more valuable than a whole battery of personality tests. Understanding the theories behind personality tests and the need for proper administration are crucial for getting better results.

---

2   Henry Cloud, John Townsend, Dave Carder, and Earl Henslin, *Unlocking Your Family Patterns* (Chicago: Moody, 2011), 117–214.

Myers-Briggs Type Indicator

The Myers-Briggs Type Indicator is based on psychological types developed by Carl Jung. This test assumes a person has multiple innate drives versus a singular innate drive. Isabel Myers was a graduate of Swarthmore College in Pennsylvania, where she became acquainted with the work of Jung. Her mother, Katharine Briggs, was also a graduate of Swarthmore. Briggs's research with children had led her to the conclusion that children possessed various personalities that could be identified.

The development of the Myers-Briggs Type Indicator set forth the following four pairs: extraversion and introversion, sensing and intuition, thinking and feeling, and judging and perceiving. The final pair, judging and perceiving, was a development of Jung's theory. Since the publication of the Myers-Briggs Type Indicator in 1944, the popularity of these tests has become widespread. The test has not been without serious criticism, however. The lack of validity of Jung's theories and even the evaluation of the Myers-Briggs test among control groups has proved to be less statistically significant than many in the general populace realize. For example, many who take the Myers-Brigg indicators can receive different results within a brief time span of test and retest.[3]

Keirsey Temperament Assessment

David Keirsey was motivated to research personality theory because of the Myers-Briggs test. Keirsey likewise was able to develop his ideas from previous writing on the subject. He differentiated between temperament, character, and personality. Temperament is the predispositional hardware on which the software of character is developed. The way the various aspects of personality hang together informs personality. Developing the work of Myers and Briggs, Keirsey observed the consistency in children over time to show the validity of his work. The pairings that Myers and Briggs developed could form many different combinations. The person is typically given a designation of four letters representing

---

3   Merve Emre, *The Personality Brokers: The Strange History of Myers-Briggs and the Birth of Personality Testing* (New York: Anchor, 2018).

their pairing. There are sixteen different combinations of these various pairings. Keirsey was able to give each of these pairings a different name. He attempted to understand how the various aspects of one's temperament would inform character and shape one's personality. The same concerns regarding the deep philosophical foundation on which the test is made are not resolved in Keirsey's development. He merely gave greater description to Myers and Briggs's initial idea.[4]

The Big Five
The Big Five is a five-factor model developed by Robert McCrae and Paul Costa. This approach was not based on Jung's work. Rather, early research in the five-factor model attempted to understand personality and temperament through a lexical analysis of how personality is described. This process occurred by identifying more than 4,500 words that described various aspects of personality. These descriptions were categorized in ever-increasing smaller units. The Big Five represents the smallest clustering of the various elements. These are extraversion, agreeableness, conscientiousness, emotional stability, and openness to experience. This matrix of personality traits or identifiers listed in the Big Five operate on a continuum. This approach is based less on a deep psychological theory and more on direct reporting and observation.[5]

DISC Assessment
William Moulton Marston originally developed the DISC assessment tool. He classified human behavior into four categories. These categories are dominance, inducement, submission, and compliance. Marston believed that while each person has more prominence in one of these categories, all are present to some degree. Marston's understanding of human behavior and personality were heavily influenced by the theoretical assumptions of both Jung and Sigmund Freud.

---

4   David Keirsey, *Please Understand Me II: Temperament, Character, Intelligence* (Del Mar, CA: Prometheus Nemesis, 1998).
5   Thomas Widiger, ed., *The Oxford Handbook of the Five Factor Model* (Oxford: Oxford University Press, 2017), 11–150, 353–80.

Marston's studies were developed into a self-assessment tool by John Cleaver in 1951 and used in the hiring process for businesses. This developed into a twenty-four-question self-assessment. The assessment remained basically unchanged until 1994, when the questionnaire was updated for greater utility. Four additional questions were added, bringing the total number of questions to twenty-eight. This tool has proved helpful in business settings to aid in greater self-awareness and bringing personality traits to light. Again, the findings of this personality assessment are as strong as the theoretical foundations it rests on, along with the accurate self-reporting of the participant.[6]

The Administration of Personality Tests

The administration of personality tests began in the 1950s, and from the 1960s onward many would begin to see the value of such tests. The administration of a personality test is dependent on several factors to glean quality results. These factors include clear instruction on the nature of the test, an understanding of the test itself, the means of scoring, and test/retest validity.

To take a personality test effectively, appropriate instructions must be given before administering the test. In many settings, a personality test is given without appropriate instruction. The availability of personality tests online has allowed pastors and church leaders to take personality tests online without the presence of an administrator. The lack of understanding of the nature of the personality test and the lack of an administrator can significantly affect results.

Conversely, it has become more commonplace to understand a cursory understanding of personality theory. Personality tests rest on the honesty of personal reporting. A person who desires a particular result can answer questions regarding their personality in a manner they believe will aid them in gaining the outcome they desire. The original psychological context of personality theory was for the purpose of self-awareness, so that a person could move toward self-actualization.

---

6   Mark Scullard and Dabney Baum, *Everything DISC Manual* (Hoboken, NJ: Wiley, 2015).

The validity of a personality test is more obvious in its consistency upon retesting. If a personality test uncovers the innate predisposition of a person, then results should remain stable over time. Retest results of the standard personality inventories have not proved stable over time. This lack of stability could be due to less than honest self-reporting or deficiencies within the test itself.[7] Pastors and church leaders will need to assess how much weight to give personality tests in understanding their personality profile.

FIXED PERSONALITY VERSUS DEVELOPED SKILLS

Personality tests are focused on the fixed personality or traits of a given person. While it is difficult to clearly identify the fixed personality of a person, there is a sense that the constitution of a person is more dominant in one trait or personality than another. While personality is more difficult to adjust, skills can be learned. It seems incorrect to rule a person out of hand for church revitalization efforts if they do not have a certain personality. Skills of revitalization can be learned and developed. A church leadership with any personality can focus on developing the needed skills to accomplish church revitalization. The following characteristics have been identified as necessary for a successful revitalization effort: visionary shepherd, tactical patience, organizational awareness, gospel orientation, missional focus, emotional intelligence, spousal perseverance, pastoral grit, resourceful generalist, initiative, affinity for multigenerational ministry, respect for church's legacy, and willingness to confront.[8]

A PLAN FOR PASTORAL WELLNESS

In addition to a pastor understanding his personality profile, he must develop a plan for personal wellness. If a pastor does not take care of

---

7   Irving Weiner and Roger Greene, *Handbook of Personality Assessment*, 2nd ed. (Hoboken, NJ: Wiley, 2017), 3–58.

8   The Replant team of the North American Mission Board has identified these characteristics as skills that can be developed within the leaders (and his spouse) to bring about church revitalization.

himself, he will be unable to take care of anyone else. Self-care is not selfishness. Often, a failure to practice adequate self-care is the result of subtle self-deception. For example, if a pastor is often run-down and exhausted due to the demands of ministry, then he might be taking too much responsibility on himself. While it is important that a pastor understand the unique and sacred calling of the pastorate, it is likewise true that Jesus is the Savior of humanity, not a pastor. If a pastor fails to complete a task, make a visit, or clearly state a biblical principle, the church of Jesus Christ will still move forward. Sadly, many pastors often realize that ministries quickly move on after their departure. So, a pastor must balance the reality of fulfilling his calling at the church where God places him with the reality that it is God's work and the congregation he serves only plays a small part in God's larger drama of redemption.

Aspects of Pastoral Wellness

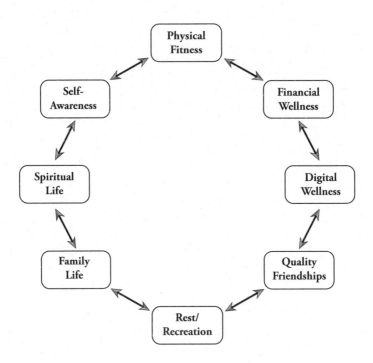

The Reality of Burnout (and Blowout)

There should be deep compassion for any pastor who has experienced burnout or is on the verge of it. The physical, emotional, and spiritual scars of burnout are long-lasting for many pastors. Without downplaying the compassion needed for pastors who burn out, a pastor also bears personal responsibility regarding burnout. Self-care is the responsibility of each person, including pastors.

Pastors must address burnout both in terms of prevention and intervention. There are many things that a pastor can do to prevent burnout. In the area of prevention, the following is simply stated but often poorly executed. First, it is important to stay in good physical shape. The influence of diet and exercise both creates greater resiliency and provides an outlet for stress. The discipline to stay at a healthy weight, eat nutritious foods, and engage in a regular workout plan should be standard for every pastor. The ability to discipline oneself regarding food and exercise should be a normative practice.

Quality community and friendship can prevent burnout. A pastor will need to develop some relationships outside the church community that he serves. There may be some within the church community who can serve as a confidante. However, a pastor needs a place to be himself. He needs friends who see him as a normal human being who experiences the full range of human emotions and receives appropriate support from them. A pastor has a responsibility to model in his own life the type of relational support and depth that he is encouraging his congregation to have with one another.[9]

A pastor must increase in self-awareness. Self-awareness is so critical in preventing burnout because a pastor should be able to identify when he has crossed an emotional line that will lead him to a bad place. A pastor should have a support system around him that puts protocols into effect when he states that he has crossed an emotional line. This author advocates for plural pastoral leadership in a church. Any pastor

---

9   Michael Todd Wilson and Brad Hoffman, *Preventing Ministry Failure: A ShepherdCare Guide for Pastors, Ministers and Other Caregivers* (Downers Grove, IL: InterVarsity, 2007), 43–64.

needs to have the flexibility to state to peers that he is moving into a bad emotional state and needs to adjust to prevent burnout.

A pastor must learn to identify the areas of ministry that drain him the most. It is interesting in ministry how seemingly small moments can take such a large emotional toll. Things are not always as straightforward as they seem. Sometimes small moments of extreme emotional toll are really the culmination of a long season of pushing through until the moment becomes too much. Also, if a pastor has unresolved emotional issues in his past, then the dynamics of a church family system can reawaken old patterns and reactivate old feelings. Therefore, a pastor will need to learn to keep boundaries around himself to prevent certain situations from taking too high an emotional toll until he is able to better understand what is happening and how he can better approach the situation. There may be a situation in which a pastor will need to distance himself from a church member or a church situation if it is creating too much disruption in him.

A pastor should be sober about the reality not just of burnout but of blowout. A blowout is typically an immoral action or a lapse of integrity. Undealt-with emotions, relational stress, and physical exhaustion all seek relief. Sometimes a pastor is unable to set back or step aside for a season out of a sense of obligation or calling. The plain reality of human personality is that our rational thoughts can only guide the process for so long. If our heart has become disordered and our feelings are regularly of despair, there will be movement toward some type of relief. If a pastor finds this momentarily outside God's Word, then the path to blowout is well on its way. The damage that this will do to a pastor and the church is great. Therefore, a pastor must resolve that God has not called him to push to the limits, so that he seeks relief from the stress outside God's commands. God never calls a pastor to this level of stress and despair. A pastor must realize that failing to set up protocols, safeguards, and realistic expectations for himself can lead to moral failure.

The Pastor and Rest and Recreation

Pastoring is a unique calling. In very few professions do people identify a person by their chosen vocation. Many church members will call their pastor by his position and not by his name. The blend of the person and the position in the pastorate is subtle. A pastor can tend to see his position as so central to his identity that he fails to internalize that who he is as a pastor and who he is as a person are two different things.

The combination of rest and recreation are two areas where a pastor can nurture his personality beyond merely serving a church. A pastor needs some time to step back from the work of the ministry to do what he enjoys. For a pastor to do what he enjoys, he must learn what he enjoys. This may be golfing, fishing, hiking, or any manner of recreation. A pastor who can see himself beyond the role of pastor is a healthier person. If a pastor's identity is primarily tied to his work, then this is a sign of unhealth. It is good for a pastor to establish a keen sense of calling into the ministry, but also to realize he only has one part to play in God's larger plan.

If a pastor is too busy to rest and recreate, then one wonders whether he is taking his ministry contribution too seriously. It is good for a pastor to be able to take a day off. Since most pastors work on Sundays, then it is good for them to take off another day of the week. Some pastors enjoy Monday because Sundays are draining, whereas others like Friday because it enables them to have a two-day weekend before Sunday. When a pastor is the only paid staff at a church, taking a day off becomes more challenging. If on his day off a pastor receives constant interruptions with church obligations such as funerals or pressing visits, then he will need to learn to take time when it presents itself. Churches are often working toward goals and objectives just like any other organization. There are times when a pastor must push hard and other times when the tasks are lighter. It is in these seasons that a pastor should seek refreshment.[10]

It is becoming more in vogue for pastors to take sabbaticals. If a pastor desires to seek a sabbatical, then he will need to work with

---

10   John Mark Comer, *The Ruthless Elimination of Hurry: How to Stay Emotionally Healthy and Spiritually Alive in the Chaos of the Modern World* (Colorado Springs: WaterBrook), 119–244.

his church to precisely determine his expectations and their expectations of him. In academic sabbaticals, a professor is to use his time to complete a significant research project. A sabbatical of this type requires intensive focus and substantial research. Many pastoral sabbaticals are more for rest and refreshment. Sabbaticals can be useful if a pastor and the church can agree on the terms of the sabbatical. However, a pastor should not overlook the importance of weekly rest and quality vacations to stave off the need for extended seasons of rest to attempt to recover from seasons that were poorly managed regarding personal care.

The Pastor and Spiritual Life

Christianity should bring about character formation. A pastor should be able to access the resources of Christianity to bring about character development. The resources of prayer, Bible intake, and Christian community are places for growth. A pastor can isolate himself from these spiritual disciplines due to the demands of church life, especially church revitalization. Church revitalization requires a pastor to focus attention on the pressing needs of the church. The building of a church ministry is different from nurturing one's spiritual life. This can be deceptive for a pastor because clearly the work of the church is a part of God's calling in the life of a pastor. The work of the church can be a crucible for the growth of spiritual maturity. Building resiliency by working through conflict, overcoming obstacles, and developing faith in difficult circumstances should result in greater maturity for a pastor. However, this only works as a pastor can keep up with personal spiritual disciplines and maintain intimacy with God through the process of church renewal.[11]

The place of a good devotional life is so necessary for this to occur. While it is important for a pastor to have a vision and well-defined goals for the church, it is also important for a pastor to have a vision and well-defined goals in his own personal spiritual life. There are

---

11 Donald Whitney, *Spiritual Disciplines for the Christian Life* (Colorado Springs: NavPress, 2014), 1–20.

differences of opinion concerning the role of a separate devotional life from the preaching ministry. For example, some pastors have a plan for Bible reading that is different from their sermon preparation. This works for many and is certainly not a bad idea. There are times that the spiritual needs of the church are different from the spiritual needs of a pastor. However, other pastors read the Bible at various levels, reading the text for the week that they will preach as the text for their own devotional nourishment. Whether or not one's devotional life and preaching schedule intertwine, it seems unwise to separate the preaching event from one's devotional life. If the goal of preaching is to apply the text to the church at large, then it seems necessary for the pastor to first apply the text to himself. If the message does not challenge and nurture the pastor, it is unlikely to challenge and nurture the congregation.

It is important as well for a pastor to know where he is in his spiritual life and develop a personalized plan for future growth. Pastors can accomplish this through reading, taking a class, participating in a Bible study, going to a conference, taking a spiritual retreat, or developing a mentorship. A pastor needs to let his own personality show, not only regarding rest and recreation but also regarding his own spiritual life. There is a real sense that a pastor's spiritual life, however connected to the life of the church, still has its own path. Hopefully, there are areas of belief and practice a pastor has mastered that he is still teaching the church. It may be too early to introduce some ideas to the church, but this does not mean that a pastor himself cannot pursue these thoughts and practices with intentionality. For a pastor to maintain spiritual health, he cannot allow his spiritual life to track directly from the difficulties of church life. If this occurs, then a pastor will not have the resources to see the church through these difficulties. If a pastor can have a spiritual life that is victorious and progressing, then he will be resourced to minister to the church. It takes great discernment to know when church life is part of a pastor's spiritual nourishment and when church life is merely the place where he ministers, receiving little in return.

The Pastor and Therapy

Many pastors are resistant to attending therapy, believing that their spiritual life should be able to help them overcome personal struggles. Many pastors, however, know too well the real struggle with depression, anxiety, burnout, and addictive behaviors. Therefore, a pastor should be open to seeking outside help especially when certain circumstances are present. It is important for a pastor to decide ahead of time which therapist he would visit and under what conditions he would require therapy. While some pastors will desire to seek a Christian counselor, other pastors will be willing to seek out a non-Christian counselor for certain issues. Again, pastors should think through these issues and settle them ahead of time. Further, it is important for a pastor not only to think through these issues personally but also to be able to provide solid advice when these types of questions arise from within the church.[12]

There are at least four circumstances under which a pastor ought to consider therapy. These include difficult life events, the persistence of problematic emotions, unresolved past trauma, and the presence of addictive behaviors.

First, the presence of difficult life events can shake any person, including a pastor. Adjustment disorders are present among people when changing life circumstances disrupt their emotional state. These can be both positive changes and negative changes. For example, a pastor moving to a new church and attempting to settle his family into a new community comes with its own struggles. Another example of a positive life event is the birth of a child. A pastor will have an adjustment within his own household and should not negate the personal effects this is having on him. Negative life events such as the death of a family member or the sickness of a spouse or child add additional levels of stress into the life of a pastor. A pastor should be aware of the need for support outside his family unit especially when these realities exist. A pastor can have a series of difficult life

---

12 David Entwistle, *Integrative Approaches to Psychology and Christianity*, 3rd ed. (Eugene, OR: Cascade, 2015), 1–190.

events that relate specifically to the ministry. For example, a pastor could have a series of funerals of prominent church members that were a loss not just to the church but to the pastor personally. Pastors ministering to families and friends of a person who has committed suicide experience a unique burden. These are situations where therapy could be warranted.

Second, a pastor needs to be open to therapy if there are persistent problematic emotions. Some pastors struggle with depression. Other pastors struggle with anxiety. The presence of problematic emotions hinders personal life enjoyment and ministry effectiveness. Many adults, pastors included, suffer from undiagnosed cases of attention deficit hyperactivity disorder or bipolar disorder. Often the cause of depression or anxiety is biological. A pastor will need to think through these issues. It seems reasonable that a pastor who discovers that he has an underlying chemical imbalance should be willing to take medication to stabilize his mood. If our biology has fallen due to sin and if medication can restore normal functioning, this certainly seems advisable within a Christian worldview. Pastors can work through the presence of problematic emotions via talk therapy and skill building. Pastors need to be able to perform simple cognitive-behavioral skills. These would include identifying irrational thoughts, stopping end-of-the-world thinking, and learning relaxation techniques. Learning these skills not only will help a pastor but will give a pastor additional skill to aid members of his congregation going through similar problematic emotions.

Third, unresolved trauma in the life of a person does not stay in the past but emerges in the present. The traumas of sexual abuse, neglect, or abandonment do not heal on their own. A pastor will need to process, grieve, and resolve them. Trauma work will require the presence of another person who is able to be with a pastor as he accesses the trauma in a safe environment to resolve it. This is a painful process and one that takes a skilled therapist to perform. Many pastors enter the ministry certainly out of a sense of calling but also out of a desire to help. A pastor should realize that sometimes this excessive need to help or save someone out of a situation is related to a past (often traumatic) event in a pastor's life in which he did not receive the help he needed. A pastor can unwittingly attempt to recreate a past trauma drama to find resolution. This, however, is not the way trauma resolves and may lead a pastor to greater and greater despair. No matter how many people a pastor helps, this will not undue the help the pastor himself failed to receive in the past.

Fourth, addiction is the clearest sign that something is wrong. However, counseling for addictive behaviors will require not only addressing the addictive (often self-soothing) behaviors themselves but also the deeper underlying condition. Further complicating the situation, pastors typically do not desire to come clean about these behaviors and will use the same tools of denial the wider public uses when addressing addictions of any sort. However, pastors need to develop accountability so that if these behaviors emerge, they can address them early. Once a pastor is deep into an addictive behavior it will be important for him to step back from ministry for a season to recover spiritual and emotional health. With appropriate self-awareness and a plan of action the mental health of the pastor can be maintained without diverting to these destructive behaviors.

Lastly, pastors in general meet a certain profile of personality. Pastors are helpers. Therefore, many of the clinical features that are present in other helping professions can be found in pastors. While helping is socially approved, it can hide underlying reasons for helping that are less than healthy. Codependent relationships are often found in dysfunctional family systems in which one person attempts to manage the negative behaviors of another.[13] Typically in codependent relationships, the one who over-gives struggles to recognize his own feelings and engages in high degrees of self-sacrifice in attempts to help or fix other people's problems. The codependent person is often bound to the emotional states of the one or ones he is attempting to help. Simply put, he cannot be okay if they are not okay. Sadly, this dynamic does not bring about health in that the codependent person

---

13   Nancy Groom, *From Bondage to Bonding: Escaping Codependency, Embracing Biblical Love* (Colorado Springs: NavPress, 1991), 15–76.

is attempting to help but enables the other person to become needier and more demanding. If this plays out in a church context, it is no wonder a pastor who is codependent would become burned or blown out due to impulsive action. If this dynamic is in play, a pastor would do well to take steps to become self-aware so that health for both him and his church is possible.

The same personality that over-gives to help and receives abuse from the congregation can be inverted. A person can believe he knows best due to divinely given knowledge and can thus be abusive to the church he serves. This can create a power relationship in which the pastor sees himself in a greater status than those he serves. This can cause the pastor to develop a messiah complex. This pastor can become very demeaning to his congregation, especially those who disagree with him. Further, he may ask those within his close circle to give unquestioned allegiance to his vision for the church. This creates a context ripe for pastoral abuse. The power balance of various relationships places the pastor in a position he should not be in. Further, the lack of accountability will allow for abusive behavior to be overlooked and covered up. These realities strongly call for a system of accountability for all pastoral staff so that these situations cannot develop in the first place.

THE PASTOR AND HIS FAMILY

The pastor has the responsibility to pastor his family well before attempting to lead a church. For younger ministers attempting to engage in church revitalization, it will be important to think carefully about the level of stress a young marriage can handle. Typically, when younger ministers attempt to engage in church revitalization the following realities are present.

First, many churches that need revitalization have older congregations, and a pastor's wife will not have a strong social system within the church for fellowship. Further, if a pastor must make a series of tough decisions, then his wife will be further isolated from the church environment. Since a pastor will need to spend a great deal of time working through church revitalization in a situation where the wife will have little or no social connection, a clear plan of action will need to be discussed and developed for community for a pastor's wife.

Second, churches in need of revitalization are typically greatly lacking in children and youth ministry. It is common for many churches in need of revitalization to think that hiring a youth pastor or young pastor is a major step toward revitalization. However, if a young pastor with children enters a church with virtually no children's ministry, his children will have to develop a plan for church involvement. A pastor will need to ask the church about his children attending another children's ministry for a season while the church develops its own children's ministry, and in general he will need to think carefully about how his family will worship together in a church that has struggled to provide ministry opportunities especially to his age group.

Third, a pastor's wife will carry the burden of church revitalization along with her husband. Therefore, it will be particularly important for a pastor to make sure his wife is on board before starting this process. If a pastor's wife is not on board and does not feel called alongside her husband to truly walk through the church-revitalization process, it would not be advisable for him to pursue church revitalization. Throughout the process of church revitalization especially as the difficult moments come, a pastor will need to keep a pulse on the well-being of his wife and children. If there is a moment when it becomes clear that the stress of church revitalization is doing too much harm to his family, then he will need to consider whether it is wise for him to continue at this ministry. A pastor needs once again to be in community and develop a communication system with leadership in the church. He should be able to set clear expectations not only for himself but also for his wife and children, and he should work out these needs on the front end. Further, if family disruption occurs because of the demands of the ministry of revitalization, then he needs to establish clear protocols on how this can be addressed proactively.

A pastor who is engaged in church revitalization is pursuing a noble goal, but he will need to be clear-eyed on how to limit negative influences on his wife and family. A pastor needs to develop a plan not just for the church to flourish but also for his family to flourish.

A pastor's family flourishing will require more than involvement in a local church, although this is an important aspect of family life. A pastor will need to think carefully if his wife is working full-time how he can support her in her job situation. If a wife is not working outside the home, how there will be ample time for emotional wellness especially if she is taking care of children? A pastor will need to plan to make sure that adequate time is open in his schedule to spend time with his wife and children. It will be important for a pastor to take adequate time off and vacation to cultivate his family life.[14]

Being a pastor of a church does not have to be a negative influence on the life of family, even in a church revitalization. If a church in need of revitalization understands the sacrifices a pastor and his family are going to have to make to see the church turn around, the church can join their team. The church and the pastor's family can develop a situation where everyone benefits. A pastor who can develop a reasonable plan that balances church work and family time and who can garner appropriate support from church leadership can find the season of church revitalization fulfilling for both the church and his family. The beauty of having an older congregation in many church-revitalization situations is that there is typically empathy and appreciation for a pastor, especially a younger pastor, who would come and give his time and energy to the church. A pastor who has developed a plan for his marriage and his children to flourish that he communicates and agrees on with church leadership has set himself up for success not only in church life but in family life as well.

THE PASTOR AND PERSONAL FINANCES

A pastor needs money to live and support his family. The pastoral ministry does not allow a pastor the luxury of working alone. The pastor's family is often involved in the ministry in some way. Therefore, the demands of ministry absorb not only the pastor's time but place various obligations on the family. Therefore, a pastor's spouse may

---

14 Daniel Langford, *The Pastor's Family: The Challenges of Family Life and Pastoral Responsibilities* (New York: Routledge, 1998), 3–72.

struggle with balancing church obligations and outside employment. Finances are a stressor for every family. Therefore, for pastors to be healthy, their financial houses need to be in order. Many within the church have various ideas regarding pastoral compensation. A pastor will need to follow these steps to attain financial wellness. First, pastors will need to develop a clear financial plan for their families to address current expenses, debt, and future goals. A pastor should take advantage of the financial literacy resources that are available.[15] Second, pastors should be honest with the church about their current financial situation and the money that they need to not only support their families but also accomplish their financial goals. Third, a pastor should seek clarity from the church on how raises and additional financial remuneration are made. In church life, working harder in the ministry does not always translate to more financial compensation. A pastor could become frustrated if additional money raised within the church is not reflected in fair, increased compensation. Therefore, as appropriate, pastors should share with the church leadership the compensation that they need to meet financial goals and find clarity on how the increased compensation will occur.

THE DIGITAL PASTOR

Digital ministry is here to stay. The digital revolution has changed so much of the way people live, including how people engage in their spiritual life. The personal struggles for pastors in digital ministry involve the digital presence of a pastor typically extending beyond a church website. The merging of personal and pastoral realities converges on one's digital presence. A pastor who is moving toward church revitalization can alienate or attract those he is attempting to reach with his online presence.

A pastor will need to decide if he desires to have a personal online presence. This would include pictures of his family, the reporting of

---

15 Dave Ramsey, *The Total Money Makeover: A Proven Plan for Financial Fitness* (Nashville: Thomas Nelson, 2003); Ron Blue, *Master Your Money: A Step-by-Step Plan for Financial Contentment* (Chicago: Moody, 2016).

life events, and expressions of his thoughts and opinions about various things. While this can help the wider congregation get to know the pastor, a pastor's online presence will be part of his public evaluation. A pastor needs to be prepared for public scrutiny of vacation pictures, days off, and pictures of the family. If a pastor is not ready for the additional exposure his online presence will bring, he needs to think carefully about what he posts. It is not negative for a pastor to have an online presence that is related to his personal family life. He may want to limit the amount of people who have access to the totality of his posts and pictures if he wants greater privacy. However, a pastor may desire to use this platform and a public/private online presence that is able to update the church community about his family life without oversharing or giving an impression he does not desire to give.

When a pastor uses his social media profile for a variety of purposes—using his personal profile to update the church on personal family issues, making comments on social issues, and offering direction and promotion of his church life—he moves into a strange in-between place. While it is true that a pastor performs all these functions personally, combining these into one social media profile is typically going to create as much difficulty as benefit. As a pastor enters the fray on a variety of social issues on his social media profile, comments and debate are likely to ensue. While a pastor's comment on some social issues will bring support from some, it will alienate others. While it is important for a pastor to speak clearly on certain social issues, one wonders if a social media profile is the best context for this to occur. Further, a pastor must stay focused on what he is attempting to accomplish. If the goal is church revitalization, spending a great deal of time and posting on social media and engaging in online arguments may not be the best use of time. A pastor needs to stay focused on ministering to the people within his church and looking for opportunities for outreach. Too often a pastor attempts to speak to a large community outside his immediate church. It is appropriate for certain figures to have a public platform, but for most pastors engaging in church revitalization, the focus needs to be on the needs of the church.

A pastor will need to work hard on developing a strategy for how the church utilizes social media. Some pastors have spoken against posting worship services on social media, arguing that the ideal is not for people to watch a worship service but to attend in person and participate. The other side of the argument is that many can get a clear glimpse of the life of the church before having to commit to attend. Whatever a church decides on the matter of posting worship services, the utilization of technology to communicate to church members and promote the ministry of the church seems to be necessary. A quality webpage, an intentional social media strategy, and a professional pastoral online presence can do a lot of good in promoting church revitalization. In many church-revitalization situations, the church is unknown (or known for the wrong things) in the community in which it is located. Social media gives an opportunity to communicate and promote the ministry of the church. A church that is going to live in the twenty-first century will need to harness social media thoughtfully and intentionally.

Why discuss pastors' digital presence in the context of overall wellness? The answer to this question is that the exposure of pastors' personal and professional lives on large social media platforms can be daunting. A pastor will be evaluated not just by the few hundred people who attend the church but by anyone who can look up the church online. A pastor's family will be evaluated on the basis of not just face-to-face interactions in the community but the pastor's online presence as well. A pastor who struggles to handle criticism will face additional spheres of criticism online and will need to utilize his social media presence accordingly.

Not only does the digital revolution allow many to see your online profile, but it makes a pastor more accessible than ever before. A pastor is reachable on his cell phone, email, social media messenger, online comments on posts, and a myriad of other ways. There are certain people who take great offense when a pastor does not respond to their attempts to reach out. A good rule here is to clearly communicate the methods people can use to reach the pastor and what the parameters of response are. This will not solve all the problems, but it will certainly be a step toward setting some reasonable boundaries. If a pastor sets the boundary that he will be primarily reachable during office hours and will respond within two business days, it will set a reasonable expectation for the church. However, if none of these boundaries are set, a pastor sets himself up to be called, emailed, and messaged through online means constantly. This will consume a great deal of time, and typically those who require a great deal of a pastor's time through these channels will not be those who are easily mobilized for ministry and push the efforts of church revitalization forward.[16] A pastor who is distracted and interrupted by his digital presence and does not use it for productive purposes will often struggle to reach his larger goals in church revitalization.

DEVELOPING A PLAN

A pastor must prioritize his own wellness and the wellness of his family if he is going to be successful in revitalization. Personal and family wellness will not occur without a plan. A pastor will need to think carefully through the following things.

First, has the pastor given sufficient reflection to personal successes and failures in his life? Writing a personal history should reveal areas of strength and weakness. Has the pastor built on past successes and overcome past struggles?

Second, has he given sufficient reflection to the successes and failures of previous pastorates? Many pastors repeat similar mistakes from pastorate to pastorate. This is difficult not only on the pastor himself but also on the churches he serves.

Third, has he realistically appraised his personality and leadership style? Has he reviewed the results of any formal personality test, with professional help and the honest feedback of those who know him best?

---

16 Amy Blankson, *The Future of Happiness: Five Modern Strategies for Balancing Productivity and Well-Being in the Digital Era* (Dallas: BenBella, 2017); Jeff Mingee, *Digital Dominion* (Leyland, England: 10Publishing, 2022); and Tony Reinke, *God, Technology and the Christian Life* (Wheaton, IL: Crossway, 2022).

Fourth, has he scheduled recreation and rest? These times allow for a pastor to do things that he enjoys unrelated to the ministry of the church. It is important for a pastor to be able to disengage from ministry work to merely engage in personal enjoyment.

Fifth, has he put protocols in place so that if he finds himself suffering from depression or anxiety he will seek counseling? A pastor must be humble enough to realize that the stress of life can put him in a bad place. Knowing when to reach out for help is not a sign of weakness but maturity.

Sixth, has he taken into consideration the effects on his family? Has he worked with his wife and children to make sure that the church environment does not bring about harm? Are there contexts outside the church that enable a pastor's wife and children to flourish?

Seventh, has he developed a plan regarding all digital means of communication so that he does not bring about undue obstacles to his ministry or open himself up to be contacted and interrupted constantly?

Pastor wellness often brings about church wellness. A pastor who has not ordered his own life and the life of his family will struggle to have the stamina for the task of church revitalization.

WHAT'S THE PLAN?

A pastor must be a leader. A clear-eyed plan for a church is essential for church revitalization. A church that needs revitalization has been unable to clearly devise and execute a quality plan for itself. This does not mean that plans are not being followed, nor that there is an absence of leaders in the church. What it does mean is the plan that has been set forth is no longer workable for the church to achieve vitality. There are many plans that can be devised to achieve church revitalization. Many churches have been able to follow different paths for vitality to be reborn. A pastor and church leadership must be able to devise a plan that is workable for a particular church in a particular season.[1] Understanding this reality means there are often fewer options for good plans, because a plan that a church will not accept and execute is not a good plan.

---

1   Aubrey Malphurs, *Advanced Strategic Planning: A 21st-Century Model for Church and Ministry Leaders* (Grand Rapids: Baker Books, 2013), 23–104.

ASSESSING READINESS FOR CHANGE

Developing a plan requires more analysis than a pastor may first realize. Not only do many churches struggle to see that the plans they are following are not really working, but when a critical mass of church members state they want revitalization, this is the first step toward revitalization, not the last. Understanding the nature of change and resistance is important when developing a plan and putting forth reasonable steps for a church. Assessing readiness for change is part of developing a plan. The less a church is ready to change, the smaller the options for change exist. A relatively minor change in a resistant church will require a lot of work and emotional energy to accomplish. Therefore, readiness for change can be evaluated in five major stages. The stages are pre-contemplation, contemplation, preparation, action, and maintenance.

Pre-contemplation is present in many declining churches. The signs of decline are so slow or are reasoned away so quickly that the church remains reasonably content in its current state. Even numerical and spiritual decline can be skewed as positive factors. A church can view itself as the last outpost for real Christians in the area or refocus itself on merely taking care of one another. This latter course is often clear when the primary function of a pastor is to make visits, care for the needs of the congregation, and sadly preach a meaningful funeral for dying members. At this point, the pastor is preparing to close the church, not revitalize it, but the members are pleased with the care they are receiving. Churches that are not ready for change in virtually any form because they have developed a workable (albeit a poor) long-term plan for the moment will just need to be given more time to change.

There are two approaches that can be employed when a church is in the pre-contemplation stage. The rock-bottom approach, which basically waits for a church to run out of money and members, will require the church to assess its situation when certain factors arise. However, it is surprising how long a church can be in the dying process yet never quite reach rock bottom. Further, when some churches finally reach rock bottom, their facilities are so in need of repair it is often easier to rebuild and start over than attempt repair. The other approach is motivational interviewing. This approach, which attempts to help the church to see beyond its immediate strategy, is difficult because it seeks to move a church that sees little need for change into contemplation for change. This is best done by a denominational leader, church strategist, or interim pastor. A pastor who is in a church that has not even begun the process of contemplating change will have to fit into the church's expectations. Therefore, a pastor in a church that is in this stage will need to be content to minister to the church in a chaplain-style ministry.

Contemplation often occurs in the most observant leaders first. The slow fade in church life can be blamed on so many external factors. Church members can decry the death of the community due to globalization, the change of demographics, the secularization of society, or bad pastoral leadership. However, even in the midst of these excuses the realities of decline are often seen in hard data such as attendance and giving records. These obvious signs allow some church members to begin to think about the need to make a change. These thoughts are often subtle. A church may contemplate initially that something of a past era needs to be reintroduced. There may be some truth to these initial thoughts, but what will make the church vital in the future is virtually never a reintroduction of an old strategy without serious modifications. This contemplation is positive, but typically the initial thoughts about how the church needs to change and how the church can look will be quite different from the end results in a revitalized church. A pastor can easily misread a situation of church contemplation, believing that because a church is thinking about change it is ready for all the changes in the mind of the leaders. This is rarely the case.

Preparation occurs when a church begins to make moves toward action. In many churches, a group of people will gather formally or informally to discuss possible changes. This process can take an exceptionally long time. Church change is often counted in months and years, not weeks. It is not unusual for a group of members in churches in need of revitalization to meet for months to discuss exceedingly minor changes. A pastor who is in this process must exercise patience. Attempting to rush church members who are accustomed to a slower pace of church life will only cause the process to slow down more.

Further, a pastor will typically need to help manage group dynamics. While a group of members may see the need for change, once preparation for any action is discussed the variety of ideas and the pace at which these ideas should be implemented will vary greatly. Not only must a pastor be aware of pushing his own agenda too hard to get the group of church members to turn against him. He must also stay on the lookout for members getting upset with one another. A pastor can be thrilled to hear that a church member sees the need for rapid change. However, if this church member is in the minority, it is possible that they will get frustrated with the process and quit. A pastor must think carefully about group dynamics so that an actionable plan can emerge out of this process. Many times, churches get to this point, have a lot of meetings, get conflicted, and abandon the process with very superficial changes that do little to engender real church revitalization.

Action occurs when a church develops plans that will work toward church revitalization. It is precisely at this point that most church-revitalization changes are often less dramatic than the level of change in a church plant. Since the church exists in some form, a pastor is not building the church from nothing. Further, good, actionable plans for church revitalization create change, but a pastor will need to likely remind himself that good church revitalization means progress, not perfection. Therefore, the goal will be to develop some initial changes toward revitalization that can be built on.

Maintenance will require that the church continue to hold these patterns of health. It is possible that after a few initial interventions, great resistance arises. The church will be pressured to go back to old forms of operation. An initial win might have stressed a portion of the congregation. Further, it is easy for a church to use a bit of vitality as an excuse to halt all progress rather than to build on it. The church, it is argued, is now stable. While it might be wise to pause if the church is stressed due to a series of changes, it would be unwise to allow for old patterns to become normative again.[2]

---

2   William Miller and Stephen Rollnick, *Motivational Interviewing: Helping People Change*, 3rd ed. (New York: Guildford, 2013), 155–302.

LOCATING THE CHURCH IN THE LIFE CYCLE

Like other organizations, churches have a life cycle. They are born, develop, mature, decline, and unfortunately die. This does not have to be the case. If churches can identify their place in the life cycle and revision, then they are able to see fresh life appear. The stages of the life cycle can be divided among many terms. For ease of communication, the terms *birth, adolescence, adulthood, plateau, decline,* and *death* will be used. There is an original purpose behind every church that is born. Starting a church is often full of excitement and unknowns. In its early years it is very fluid, often formed around a small group of people with limited purposes. As a church grows into adolescence, systems and processes must be put in place for internal alignment and external outreach. Eventually a more clearly aligned organizational structure and system are established. The church reaches adulthood and has come to age in its organization. Reaching maturity as an organization means that systems and structures are developed for more complex functions. However, the systems and structures that can lead a church toward health in one era are the very systems and structures that can lead to decline in another.

Church Life Cycle

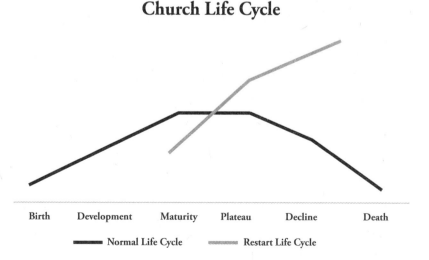

Birth   Development   Maturity   Plateau   Decline   Death

━━━ Normal Life Cycle   ▬▬▬ Restart Life Cycle

A plateau and subsequent decline are subtle. It is often difficult for a church to believe that plateau and decline are happening because the systems and protocols are being followed precisely. The problem is these systems and protocols no longer meet the needs of the moment. Times change, the situation is different, but the strategy is the same. This is a difficult moment because it involves a push and pull of change and control. There are some who realize the church must become less structured to adjust to the moment, and there are those who will resist any change to the structure. Here the church can be consumed internally with conflict, even attempting to undo old structures. A church that has grown old has a tough time acting young again. However, this is what is required. The old systems and processes must be readdressed, and a new vision that meets the moment must be developed and implemented to move the church to an earlier phase in the lifecycle. If this does not occur, a church can remain in a stable or plateaued position for years, even decades. However, without addressing the lifecycle realities death will ensue at some point in the future. It can be a slow, agonizing death, or it can occur quickly.[3]

Locating a church in the life cycle will have substantial influence on what interventions toward church revitalization are possible. If a church has merely been through a difficult season, clarity of vision and realignment of resources can make church revitalization doable. However, if decline has been ongoing, then significant work must be done for the revitalization effort to be possible. A church that has been in decline for several years may or may not have the necessary resources to accomplish revitalization.[4] A church must not only develop a plan for revitalization but must also have the required resources to execute the plan developed.

---

3   Bill Henard, *ReClaimed Church: How Churches Grow, Decline, and Experience Revitalization* (Nashville: B&H, 2018), 7–104.

4   Les McKeown, *Predictable Success: Getting Your Organization on the Growth Track—and Keeping It There* (Austin: Greenleaf, 2010), 95–130.

FOSTERING

Churches that have experienced decline over a substantial period may not have the resources to be able to execute a revitalization effort. Fostering is a process by which another church aids a struggling church with necessary coaching and resources to aid in the revitalization effort. A fostering church is not seeking to make the church part of their ministry. Rather, the fostering church comes alongside the struggling church for a limited time (typically one to two years) for the purpose of helping the church retain autonomy and supplementing resources for the revitalization effort. If fostering is successful, the struggling church will gain strength and continue revitalization on its own. If fostering is unsuccessful, the struggling church will need to decide either to close or replant.[5]

COMMON STRATEGIES IN CHURCH REVITALIZATION

While each church has a unique situation that needs to be carefully taken into consideration, there are some common initial strategies that can help a church take its first actionable steps toward revitalization. It is important to know some of these initial interventions so that their effectiveness for a particular situation can be evaluated. It is possible to do more than one intervention at a time. However, attempting to do too much too fast may frustrate the process. Even in a multifaceted approach, these interventions will need to be scheduled out in an orderly fashion, so the church has clarity on each task at the proper time.

Prayer-Focused Revitalization

Prayer is the catalyst of spiritual renewal. This intervention is a nonnegotiable even if other interventions are utilized. Prayer for church renewal is different from church members praying about

---

5   North Carolina Baptists are to be commended for their process of church fostering as a major tool in church revitalization. They have developed a workable process for the churches in their state.

the needs in their life. Prayer for church renewal brings the church together for focused prayer around the needs of the church. Church members are encouraged to specifically pray for the church, pray for the lost, pray for leaders in ministry, pray for the pastoral staff, pray for the deacons, and pray for clarity and greater vision for the church. Many churches that pray can fail to pray specifically for God to do a work in the church. When the entire church is committed to pray for the spiritual needs of the church and community, God can move in greater ways.[6]

Worship-Based Revitalization

The largest gathering of the church every week is typically the corporate worship service. If a church does not offer a quality worship service, it is hard for a church to be revitalized. Worship-based revitalization attempts to think through and improve the overall Sunday morning experience. While the music and the message will be important, there is more to worship-based revitalization than merely these two aspects. Churches that offer a quality worship service think about the entire worship experience. There are simple touches that communicate to the church that worship is important. These features can include greeters at main entrances, quality printed materials such as a bulletin, and a clean facility, especially the bathrooms and nursery area.

Regarding the worship service, there needs to be an attempt at planning. While a worship service should not be fully scripted, there certainly does need to be a sense of intentionality. Announcements need to be well crafted, music needs to be offered to the best of the church's ability, prayer needs to be personalized to church needs, and the message needs to be prayerfully prepared. These simple acts of intentionality signal to the church that an attempt at revitalization is underway. The more difficult but often necessary aspects of worship-based revitalization occur when the worship service needs

---

6   Thom Rainer, *Anatomy of a Revived Church: Seven Findings on How Congregations Avoided Death* (Spring Hill, TN: Rainer Publishing, 2020), 71–84.

WHAT'S THE PLAN?   141

to be adjusted to minister more effectively to a wider audience. This may mean changing service order, updating the music, adjusting a preaching style, and potentially bringing new participants into worship. Even if done with discernment, these changes may still be resisted by some, but they may also reach out to a wider group. In a revitalization, a pastor will need to discern whether changing the worship should be the first actionable move toward revitalization.[7]

Evangelism-Focused Revitalization
The failure to share the gospel leads to spiritual dryness. A fresh focus on evangelism can certainly aid in revitalization. While older models of sharing the gospel are not as useful as in past generations, gospel sharing is still a mandate for all Christians. If a church engages in basic training in sharing the gospel, calls members to merely share the gospel with one person and gives the church tools to aid in a simple gospel presentation, church vitality can emerge from this context. Evangelism in many American contexts must build a greater bridge because the basic presuppositions of the Christian faith are not as widely held. There is growing disbelief in the existence of God, the reality of sin, divine judgment, and divinely offered personal salvation. Evangelistic engagement may take more time to address these concerns and require a greater relational commitment. However, the evangelistic response may be more solid because those who come to faith will do so out of a greater understanding of the gospel. If a church is ready to share the gospel, the potential for church revitalization is great.[8]

Small-Group-Based Revitalization
Small groups both enable the deepening of relationships within the church and serve as an opportunity for outreach outside the

---

7   Tom Cheyney, *38 Church Revitalization Models for the 21st Century* (Orlando: Renovate, 2014).
8   Ed Stetzer and Mike Dodson, *Comeback Churches: How 300 Churches Turned Around and Yours Can Too* (Nashville: B&H, 2007), 76–160.

church. New small groups can be formed with little disruption to the current state of church life. Further, if a church has an aging congregation, a young couple can form a new small group to reach younger couples within the community without the initial struggle of bringing them into an older congregation. Further, a good small group offers an opportunity for deepening relationships. Many small groups meet in a member's home. This personal setting creates a different type of interpersonal atmosphere. This is not to rule out the possibility that the same objectives cannot be accomplished through more traditional Sunday school programs. The difficulty of small-group revitalization occurs when the new growth or the vitalized members in the church face resistance from those who do not see the need for change within the church. If a small group is reaching new people, the introduction of these families into the life of the church should be met with joy. However, sometimes the presence of a new contingent of people is directly or indirectly viewed as a threat to old power networks. However, if vitalized members and new members can assimilate into the life of the church, this can cause fresh vitality.[9]

Catalytic-Event-Based Revitalization

Catalytic-event-based revitalization attempts to create quick momentum using an event. This event is typically community-focused. These could be as simple as a community block party. The point of a catalytic event is to communicate to the surrounding community that the church is operational and ready to serve the community. Reports on the effectiveness of event-based revitalization are mixed. Many pastors and churches look for an immediate return from the catalytic event. For example, a small church may have a community block party that attracts hundreds, but the following Sunday church attendance is the same. Some pastors decry the willingness of the

---

9   Kenneth Priest and Alan Stoddard, *Groups That Revitalize: Bringing New Life to Your Church through Sermon-Based Small Groups* (Littleton, CO: Acoma, 2019), 45–102.

community to participate in community events but then failing to come to church. This appears to misunderstand the process of revitalization. Seen from another perspective, a positive experience for the community at a church event is an especially important win. Further, many who attend church events may have had a bad church experience or are merely testing out the church experience. A pastor or church should not expect an immediate return on investment. The church must commit to ministering to the community in fresh ways and use each one of these community events to build relationships and earn trust. Event-based revitalization can be a straightforward way to get the church outside the walls of the building. However, expectations will need to be tempered so that the church does not expect one positive experience with the church to overturn years of church stagnation or to overcome a past church hurt.

New Leadership Revitalization

New church leadership offers a unique opportunity for church revitalization. The presence of new pastoral staff and even new leadership structures can aid in revitalization. If a church needs revitalization, there has been a lack of leadership and a lack of congregational support to move the church toward vitality. Once patterns of behavior between church leadership and a congregation are set in place, it is difficult to change. It is possible for a current pastor to reform his leadership style so that he encourages the church toward greater revitalization. However, it is easier for a pastor who does not have a history with the church to change the way things operate and to introduce a new form of leading.

Next-Generation Revitalization

Reaching the next generation is important for the vitality of a church. A robust children's and student ministry typically signals the presence of vitality. However, older congregations will need to be willing to do a lot to reach and retain the next generation. Many churches pursuing revitalization realize the need to reach children, students, and young families. However, this will not be done by merely adding a program onto the current structure. To be welcoming to a younger audience, change will need to occur on many fronts. Whether the church realizes it or not, it is set up to attract exactly who it is attracting. Therefore, hiring a children's or youth pastor and starting a new program will not create the level of cooperation to truly reach the next generation. A church must be willing to invest in the next generation while at the same time offering a total church experience that is more conducive to the group they are attempting to reach.

Multisite-Based Revitalization

The multisite church revolution continues to grow and flourish. The model of one church in many locations is still developing. While for many churches it is ideal to keep their autonomy, this is not viable for many churches. Some church facilities are in strategic places and are in proximity to another vital work. In cases like that it might be better for a church to merge into another work than to die. The merging of a church facility to be the site of another church typically means the church loses it old identity to take on the characteristics and mission of the mother church. This will require humility, patience, and openness to the philosophy of the mother church. Sometimes the mother church will allow the pastoral staff to remain in the church in a nonteaching role. This can be done successfully, but a church will need to relinquish authority to the church that is willing to bring them on as part of a multisite campus.[10]

Restart/Replant-Based Revitalization

Sometimes church revitalization will mean giving away the church property to a new work. This approach is basically providing a

---

10   Geoff Surratt, Greg Ligon, and Warren Bird, *The Multi-site Church Revolution: Being One Church in Many Locations* (Grand Rapids: Zondervan, 2006), 45–59.

church planter and his team an older facility to start a new work. In cases like this, when the change required is unlikely to occur, the church offers up its property with the current congregation and another vital congregation utilizes the space. For churches like this, some recommendations must be heeded. Basically, in this model the main offering of the church is to provide a building. If the church is not thoughtful in the gifting of a building even this final strategy can fail. Typically, a church that has been declining for years has a lot of deferred maintenance. Further, monetary reserves are usually taken down to virtually zero before a church is willing to transfer the property to another work. A church undergoing these circumstances may be less attractive to a church plant than purchasing a new building. Ideally, churches that realize they need a new work to accomplish a replant must be proactive in transferring the property. In an ideal situation, the church will attempt to address major deferred maintenance issues before they devalue the building greatly. Also, it would be ideal for a church to gift some money to a new church plant to make the gifting of the building more attractive. If a church plant had an older building without major deferred maintenance issues and $50,000, it would be more probable that the new church would thrive in that location.[11]

BEST PRACTICES IN REVITALIZATION

There are common best practices in revitalization. While in one sense, every church-revitalization situation is unique, they all have some similar features. It is important to note what is similar in various church-revitalization situations so these features can become part of the unique plan for church revitalization.

Culture of Excellence

A culture of excellence is essential to the execution of a plan. Whatever steps toward revitalization a church pursues, the initiatives must

---

11   Mark Hallock, *Replant Roadmap: How Your Congregation Can Help Revitalize Dying Churches* (Littleton, CO: Acoma, 2017), 23–58.

be carried out with excellence. Attention to detail, quality execution of initiatives, orderliness, and going above and beyond expectation can make any plan attractive. A great plan done without excellence has poorer chances of success. The leadership team needs to commit to excellence. Further, a culture of excellence is put in place not only in the initial implementation of a plan but in each stage of all initiatives. Striving for constant improvement will set a pace for quality implementation and continual quality improvement.

Disposition of Leadership

Church leadership must have crystal clarity on the plan they desire to implement. However, the disposition of church leadership will need high degrees of emotional intelligence. The pacing, interventions chosen, ability to pause, ability to listen, ability to stand firm, and the ability to compromise require a unique disposition of leadership. Strong leaders can develop a plan and implement it at all costs. While this works in some business settings where there is understood allegiance to a leader, it often fails in a church environment. If it does succeed, a portion of the church typically retreats or leaves the church. In an environment where the church is too small to withstand such trauma, the entire church may be deeply harmed. And typically, this type of strong leader leaves. The ability of church leadership to have a clear plan and simply deal with the lack of strategic movement of some church members requires unique patience and maturity. However, it is often this type of leader who can survive the process of church revitalization.

Affirming Measured Growth and Acceleration

Church leadership must not only have a unique disposition of patience and strategy implementation but also execute measured growth. Everything does not need to be completed within the first few years. Successful church leadership must realize that church decline has taken years to materialize, and that revitalization will take time as well. Therefore, initial plans must not overwhelm the congregation but must be seen by the church as doable and reasonable. While a church congregation may need to trust God for what he can do in church revitalization, church leadership must realize that there have been years of stagnations and that God's power has not been observed in the life of the church. Therefore, wise church leadership demonstrates to the church small wins and then builds on these small wins to generate momentum for greater interventions in the future.

Budgetary Alignment

A church in need of revitalization typically has limited resources. The resources have been allocated in a way that produced the current situation. There is little extra money in a church in need of revitalization. While not everything requires money, some interventions will require some budget to see them accomplished. Church leadership can get buy-in on budgetary alignment to make the limited resources of the church better positioned to accomplish plans that can encourage revitalization. Church leadership in a revitalization will also function as fundraisers. Resources are typically a major obstacle in church revitalization. Church members are often willing to give to vision. The lack of vision for the church has typically been one of the many reasons the church has not been compelled to give more sacrificially to the ministry of the church.

Facility Enhancement for Ministry Effectiveness

The state of many church facilities is a visual representation of the state of the church. When members and visitors alike enter the building, the carpet from thirty years ago, the dirty bathrooms, the outdated nursery, and the poor sound system all communicate the state of the church. The facilities communicate that the church is in need of vitality. Rehabilitating a building that has experienced years of deferred maintenance is a daunting task. However, a visual sign of freshness in a church facility can communicate to the church that church revitalization is underway. An area of the church that has been a long-term eyesore can especially be an area that the congregation is motivated to fix and give toward. Again, updating a facility will not in and of itself cause revitalization, but often some facility improvement signals to the church that church revitalization is in motion.

A Simple Path to Discover Vision

Discovering the vision of the church can be a long, complicated process. Some churches distribute surveys, form groups, have meetings, and expend a lot of energy in a visioning process. Some of this process will be necessary. However, discovering the vision of the church is both simple and complex. Many church members can envision a more vibrant church than the one that currently exists. Rather than attempting to craft a perfect vision for the church, just developing and agreeing on a better vision can move the church toward revitalization. Since the actual process of church revitalization is going to take a lot of energy, it is important not to overexpend energy in the planning phase of revitalization. Therefore, a simple path to discover vision without frustrating the church in the initial planning phase is especially important for successful implementation.[12]

MAKING YOUR CONVICTIONS PLAIN THROUGH VISION

A vision is a compelling future reality that calls the church to action. It is important to remember that while the church will need a step-by-step approach to accomplishing a future desired state, the vision cannot merely aim for the head. It must also aim for the heart. A compelling vision enables the church to see afresh what they can be. This vision will need to enable church members to see a church that is cultivating strong community, reaching a younger generation, nurturing Spirit-led worship, and reversing the effects of years of decline.

Before a church attempts to dream again and aspire to make the church greater than its current state, the church needs to evaluate why it will aspire to attempt church revitalization. Hopefully, the reason a church would attempt church revitalization is because of a deep desire to serve God and make disciples. The why of church revitalization is a desire to see God's glory revealed in every church. The presence of

---

12 Thom Rainer, *Breakout Churches: Discover How to Make the Leap* (Grand Rapids: Zondervan, 2005), 91–164.

a dying church is out of step with God's victorious plan. Therefore, the recovery of God's glory in every declining church should be a strong motivating factor.

VISION STATEMENT, MISSION STATEMENT, AND VALUES

A vision statement is for the purpose of aspiration. It paints a picture of a future desired state. A vision for a church could be a desire to touch every home in the city or to engage missions or to focus on the community. These are aspirational statements that provide a framework for a future reality. A vision statement does not require all the specific details to be described. It calls the church to action emotionally by envisioning a future for the church that is the basis for motivation.

A mission statement provides objectives for the purpose of the church's existence. Many churches' mission statements revolve around the commands of Jesus to love God and neighbor or to make disciples. A mission statement gives clarity on the objectives of a church and can serve as a guiding principle for everything accomplished in the church. A pastor could use the mission statement as the means to evaluate the programs of the church. If a church's ministries are poorly aligned with the mission statement of the church, then church leaders should address those ministries. Ideally, every ministry of the church should fulfill the objective set forth by the mission statement. If ministries of the church do not achieve the objectives of the mission statement, it is worth asking how these ministries are contributing to the objectives of the church.

The values of a church are a further elaboration on how the mission statement will be accomplished—for example, the means by which a church seeks to make disciples. The values of a church, like the marks of the church discussed in chapter 2, could be evangelism, discipleship, worship, fellowship, prayer, and ministry. These values engage the mind, motivate the heart, and create action, further elucidating the mission statement and providing greater clarity to accomplish the objectives of the mission statement. Further, the values clarify the parameters of how the church can accomplish the mission of the church.[13]

THE PROBLEM WITH BEING UNSPECIFIC

The process of change is a time of vulnerability for a church. The church knows how to operate under the old plan, so clarity regarding the new plan is essential. It builds confidence and competency. A pastor can believe that he has achieved clarity while the congregation feels otherwise. This lack of clarity is due to two main factors. First, the plan itself is not clear enough. There are many assumptions a pastor can make about a plan that are not assumed by the congregation. Therefore, every detail of a plan must be mapped out. The diligence of clear plan-making is a very consuming project. Second, the plan itself might be clear, but it is not communicated clearly enough. About the time pastors, church leadership, and staff are weary of discussing a plan is often the time the congregation is just beginning to comprehend it. A pastor should not underestimate how hard it is to get people to understand the contours of the most basic plan. This is not due to the lack of intelligence of the congregation, but the divided attention in their lives. A church member has many obligations. Therefore, church is often a solace from the hectic schedule. It requires mental work to think about strategy as it relates to church life, and this requires focused intentionality by church leadership.

Developing a clear plan is a mix of aspirational and actual goals. If a plan is merely a sterile step-by-step process without a clear end goal, it will not motivate the heart. If a plan is merely aspirational it should have enough focus on the details of execution to accomplish it. A long tenure for a pastor in a church is ten years. The average tenure of a pastor in a church is around four years. Developing actual plans beyond five to ten years is an exceedingly difficult prospect. However, to achieve church revitalization a pastor must commit to stay at a church for the long-term to see deep change realized. The ability to dream and execute actionable steps toward church revitalization is essential for a quality plan.

---

13 Michael Worth, *Nonprofit Management: Principles and Practice*, 5th ed. (Thousand Oaks, CA: Sage, 2019), 186–88.

Developing a Plan

Five- to Ten-Year Aspirational Goals

What is the best-case scenario for the church in five to ten years? Develop the vision of what this would look like.

Five-Year Actual Goals

List actual goals that must be accomplished for the aspirational goal to occur over the next five years. Write out goal and action plan.
1. Goal 1 (with detailed plan of action)
2. Goal 2 (with detailed plan of action)
3. Goal 3 (with detailed plan of action)
4. Goal 4 (with detailed plan of action)
5. Goal 5 (with detailed plan of action)

One-Year Aspirational Goals

What is the best-case scenario for the church in the upcoming year?

One-Year Actual Goals

List actual goals that must be accomplished for the aspirational goal to occur in the next year. Write out goals and action plans.
1. Goal 1 (with detailed plan of action)
2. Goal 2 (with detailed plan of action)
3. Goal 3 (with detailed plan of action)
4. Goal 4 (with detailed plan of action)

Five- to Ten-Year Aspirational Goals

Aspiration goals are not goals that need clarity on how a church will accomplish them, but merely a vision of what a church could be. It is important to avoid asking questions about feasibility of accomplishing aspirational goals, but to merely dream what could be. A pastor starting his pastorate at a church could ask what he would like his legacy to be at this place. What does he hope the church will have become upon his exit? Further, especially in church-revitalization situations, a past era seemed to have more vitality than the current one. It is helpful to ask members to express how the realities of the past era could be realized in the future. For example, maybe a church was known for its mission involvement, worshipful music, or evangelistic outreach.

Get members to express how this would look if it were recovered. Allow new members in a church revitalization to express what aspects of other churches they envision their church obtaining. Again, it is important to stay focused on expressing aspirational goals without attention to detail and feasibility.

Aspirational goals sometimes feel unreachable, but part of the reason the church has not reached for them is because they have become overly fixated on obstacles and immediate feasibility. In the field of counseling, counselors ask clients the miracle question. The miracle question asks the client to pretend that tomorrow morning when you awake the problems of life are gone. Then the therapist asks the client to describe what this problem-free life looks like. Likewise, when talking about aspirational goals, the church merely contemplates that if the church were as they hope it to be, what would it look like? Many church members have general aspirations and hope for the church, but these are rarely articulated in specific ways. Further, what many church members have given up as impossible is far more doable than they realize when they finally state their aspirations.

Five-Year Actual Action Steps

The movement from aspirational to specific action steps is simple. If an aspirational goal is going to be accomplished, then certain steps would need to be taken to realize it. It is important to carefully state three to five major things that must be accomplished in the next five years to reach the aspirational goal. These action steps must be placed in some type of sequence. Depending on the action steps, they may need to occur either concurrently or one after the other. A leadership team can solidify what these action steps need to be. Even at this point it is not necessary to work out the detail of how each one will be completed. Each action item will need to be clearly stated. The details as to how to best accomplish them can be worked out later.

One-Year Aspirational Goals

As you are in this planning process, it becomes easier when a leadership team thinks only in terms of one year. One year is a truly short period in the life of a church. However, if a leadership team envisions how the church could have its best year ever, ideas about what would be accomplished at the end of one year is still aspirational. Just dreaming about how the church could have its best year will engage robust conversation and excitement. It is important again that the feasibility of the aspirations is not evaluated at this point. The door is open to allow for brainstorming.

One-Year Actual Action Steps

This is the arduous work of planning in church revitalization. What are the minimum of one and maximum of four actions steps that will be accomplished this year to see the one-year aspirational goal accomplished or partially realized? These one-year objectives need to be consistent with the long-term vision of the church. However, they need to be short-term enough to be accomplished in one year in order to gain a short-term win that is consistent with the long-term vision of the church. Getting wins in the short term can build momentum and energy to increase in scope and speed on future initiatives. If a church is not able to gain a few short-term wins to show that aspirational goals can at least be partially realized, there will not be sufficient motivation to continue to push the vision forward.

These clearly developed action steps must state the what, the who, and the how. What is going to be accomplished must be written with crystal-clear detail. Who is going to see to it that these plans are implemented and must be organized with crystal-clear detail? How it is going to be accomplished must be administrated with crystal-clear detail. This must be first understood and communicated to the church leadership team, but once it is developed it must be clearly communicated to the church at large.[14]

MANAGING THE PROCESS OF CHANGE

Change is not nearly as difficult as the change process. A good leader not only has to know where he is going but must also manage the

---

14 Will Mancini and Warren Bird, *God Dreams: 12 Vision Templates for Finding and Focusing Your Church's Future* (Nashville: B&H, 2016), 39–72.

church through the process of change. For example, a freshly renovated home is a wonderful end goal. However, living in a house that is under renovation is not nearly as enjoyable. Likewise, a church that is in a change process will go through a season that may be less enjoyable than the current state of things so that a new future reality can be realized. A pastor who is not able to empathize with this reality may compromise the possibility of change.[15] Communication, understanding, restatement of vision, restatement of actionable steps, and the ability to make the change process as enjoyable as possible are important. A pastor must focus on managing today while making tomorrow better. Some will not be up for the journey no matter how much encouragement the pastor gives. Therefore, he will need to embrace the reality that some will not make the journey, but ought to graciously allow them to depart the church with an open door for them to return in a different season. A pastor also during this time needs to appreciate the leaders and members who are walking through this process. This can be accomplished through appreciation dinners, letters and emails of encouragement, and spoken words of encouragement. A pastor will need to be a positive cheerleader and empathic listener as the change process unfolds.

COMMUNICATE, COMMUNICATE, COMMUNICATE

It is hard to overstate the need to communicate. Communication must be frequent, succinct, detailed, and passionate. It is better for the church to become tired of hearing the vision than for them to be confused about what the vision is. It is easy to give a three- to five-minute update and restatement of the vision immediately before the Sunday morning message, while keeping in mind that it can become problematic if *all* messages are about the church vision. Church leaders must communicate the vision often through various

---

15 Jeff Iorg, *Leading Major Change in Your Ministry* (Nashville: B&H, 2018). Iorg gives personal testimony on the emotional toll of leading people through the change process before experiencing the joys of positive change.

means—for example, handouts and social media. One simple handout can set forth what is occurring in the life of the church over the next year. Therefore, anyone who is confused about what is happening can read the vision as well as hear the vision.

Succinct vision communication is also necessary. While there are times to say more, many times the need is to say less. The vision of the church should be able to be simply stated in one minute or less. It will be these small summaries of the vision that will give many in the church a simple grasp of what is going to be accomplished. Once a communicator can make a vision simple, it often means that the communicator truly has internalized the vision.

Details should be given occasionally. A few in the church will often desire more detail. It is important for church leadership to be transparent about the details of the vision. Even in places where accomplishing the vision will require the church to be stretched, it is prudent to be honest to the church about this reality. Further, when it comes to spending church money, it is important to be forthcoming about how money is spent, and decisions are made. This will not be necessary for everyone in the church, but necessary for some. Therefore, clear, detailed responses to honest questions should be met with competence to engender confidence in church leadership.[16]

Passion and urgency are so important in communication.[17] The church needs to know if a pastor merely knows the vision or if he believes in the vision. Passion communicates a pastor's belief in the vision. When clear vision and passion meet there is virtually always a group willing to follow and participate in the vision. Passion cannot merely be short-lived. It is especially important as the change process unfolds and difficulties arise that a pastor maintain passion and optimism. The church will need a pastoral staff that is able to show optimism and passion through the change process.

---

16 Chip Heath and Dan Heath, *Switch: How to Change Things When Change Is Hard* (New York: Currency, 2010), 101–249.

17 John Kotter, *A Sense of Urgency* (Boston: Harvard Business Review Press, 2008), 1–38.

MAKING YOUR PLAN
CONTEXTUAL AND POSSIBLE

It is important to understand context when communicating and implementing the vision, and it is important to know the people. If a pastor thinks he will communicate a vision like another pastor at another church or mimic goals and objectives of another church, it will likely fail. The vision for the church must be the vision appropriate for the church in this location. Further, the people in the church need to receive communication in a certain way. Communication and implementation need to consider the history of the church, the personality of the church, the cultural location of the church, and a myriad of other factors. The plan must fit the church and the personalities of those in the church. For this reason, when developing a plan, make sure the plan is not just possible in theory but in the culture in which the church is located. This is often as simple as talking to the church about the plan informally. Sometimes the vision needs to marinate informally in the church for a season before it can or should be promoted publicly. A church leadership team wants to set itself up for success. So, a church may require informally setting forth ideas, listening, compromising, and persuading for a season before the church is ready to participate in a revitalization plan.

CHAPTER 7

WHO'S THE TEAM?

The task of church revitalization is a team effort. Even in church models where a singular leader may have more prominence, a team is always required. It is not enough to have a good plan without a good team. The plan must be clear, and the team must be organized. In churches there are varieties of leadership. Therefore, understanding the varieties of leadership and coordinating these leaders toward common objectives are critical tasks.[1]

One of the common mistakes among pastors is developing a decent plan but failing to develop and organize a team. Therefore, the pastor sets out to implement a plan without help. There are always leaders in the church. If a pastor surprises the leaders of the church with a plan, he can expect apathy at best and resistance at worst. With a clear-eyed vision of leadership organization, a plan can be implemented swiftly while managing the resistance in the church.

---

1   James M. Kouzes and Barry Z. Posner, eds., *Christian Reflections on the Leadership Challenge* (San Francisco: Jossey-Bass, 2004), 85–98.

CHURCH LEADERSHIP TEAMS

In every church there is a top tier of leadership. This could be a solo senior pastor or a group of elders. Plurality of leadership seems to be the most faithful to the biblical text and practical for mutual input and accountability. However, defining the top tier of church leadership will be necessary.

Organizing a Team

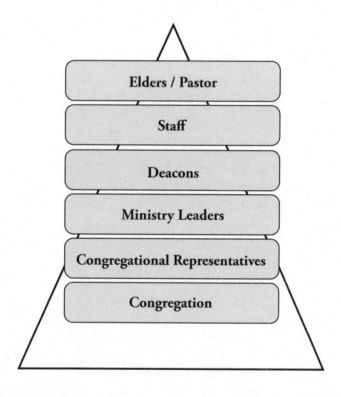

Pastoral Leadership

A major function of the office of pastor is the responsibility for oversight. It should be clear who is designated with the responsibility for overseeing the church and giving it guidance. While many leaders will be responsible for their area of ministry, the office of pastor is given the responsibility for the oversight of the entire church. Churches that affirm elder-based government often have paid and nonpaid elders. Therefore, a pastor or pastoral staff can devote more time to ministry work than nonpaid elders. Also, churches that have multiple pastoral staff members do not place all of these in senior leadership positions. For example, in some churches the youth pastor would not be on the senior leadership team even though he is full-time staff.

Defining which paid, full-time staff serve on the senior pastoral leadership team is important. Those who are full-time and on the senior leadership team will bear more leadership tasks than those who are on the leadership team but are not paid. Many churches have a mix of paid and nonpaid senior-level leaders.

The person who has the most face time with the congregation will naturally be seen as an important leader. It will be the responsibility of the pastoral staff that has the most face time with the congregation to state the leadership of the church. Further, it will be important that a pastor use opportunities of face time with the congregation to lead the church, but not to the extent that it overshadows the other leaders of the church. A pastor should use his leadership to highlight other leaders within the church and show how the entire church is working together on a church-revitalization plan.

Elder Affirmation

In church models with a plurality of elders, there is still variety. In some models, the lead pastor is understood as a leader among equals. In other models, each elder is understood as equal and someone other than the main teaching pastor or pastors is given the task of organizing and running elder meetings. It is important to understand that once one has developed a theological conviction about church leadership, there are many practical realities that need clarifying. Stating whether a church is pastor-led, elder-led, deacon-run, or congregationally governed does not resolve questions about how the church operates under such governing models.

Among the senior leadership of the church, there must be clarity and affirmation of the plan. A pastor within a church will need to press the need that all senior leadership must commit to the plan without reservation. If there are reservations, they will need to be voiced and worked through in private before presenting a plan to the church. Further, a pastor should not be surprised if senior leadership commits to a plan behind closed doors and then in the push-and-pull of congregational life reneges on the plan. If a leader is not firm on his decisions, he is not ready for high-level leadership. A pastor will need to be wise in leading all senior leadership to formally commit to a plan. This might mean writing the outline of the plan and then leading all senior leadership to sign it showing their commitment to it. It is the reality of leadership that if a person is not asked to formally commit to a plan, it is easier to distance from it when the plan meets resistance.

It is important for each leader at the senior level to have a role in presenting, communicating, and implementing the church-revitalization plan. Church leaders must often make tough decisions when moving through a church-revitalization process. A nonpaid leader with a history in the church can be invaluable, especially in difficult moments, if he has affirmed the plan. There are few people who understand the deep church dynamics, hidden resistance, and operations of a church like a long-term member.[2] A new pastor would be wise to recruit several members like this on his team, so the burden of leadership and communication does not fall squarely on his shoulders. A united front of leadership filled with leaders who have the congregation's respect is a first step in developing a high-quality team.

Defining the Leadership Team's Scope of Leadership (Oversee, Do Not Micromanage)

In a church-revitalization situation, there are many structures that are broken. In a good organization, decisions for certain tasks can be passed down to other groups. However, in churches that have stagnated, the decision-making process is cumbersome and the ability to implement plans is low. A leadership team ready to make changes

---

2   Gene Getz, *Elders and Leaders: God's Plan for Leading the Church* (Chicago: Moody, 2003), 237–324.

can quickly start accomplishing the plan. This might be necessary for a brief period; however, a leadership team needs to learn how to lead rather than micromanage. To competent leaders, this can be a frustrating process as other members in the church struggle to perform tasks they are given. This is where leading becomes incredibly necessary. Leaders within the church come alongside the church to equip, train, help, and grow others. This will be slower in the short term but will pay dividends in the long term. Further, if senior-level leadership begins to do all the work, the congregation will not believe it is their vision to implement. Therefore, they will be extremely passive and slow the process.

The Need to Lead Leaders

The church's senior leadership should attempt to achieve wins even when utilizing other leaders within the church. Wise leaders can realize which groups within the church are going to be resistant or reluctant to change. While it is important to communicate to this group, it is unwise to attempt to get them to align and participate with the vision first. This group will likely be resistant and need to see things working before they will join in the effort.

It is important to identify other leaders within the church who can see the vision and provide them responsibilities to implement it. The leaders of the church need to show they can lead others to accomplish the plan. Leading is not leading if no one is following, so this quality of leadership will need to be demonstrated early in the process of church revitalization.[3] In many churches there are ministry teams or committees. It is important to find these structures that still have vitality or the possibility of vitality and allow them to share in the leading.

The Need to Develop and Recruit Leaders

All the leaders the church needs to flourish may not be in the church. Some within the church could lead with greater development, or they

---

3   Aubrey Malphurs, *Being Leaders: The Nature of Authentic Christian Leadership* (Grand Rapids: Baker Books, 2003), 13–172.

may be outside the church. A good leader looks for those within the church who have potential for leadership. It is fulfilling to watch when those who are not leading at a high capacity are invited to take on greater leadership, and how so many rise to the occasion. Leaders can be developed by giving people greater scope of leadership or spending time with them to train them for new leadership tasks. A good leader within a church will always be looking for those who could do more.

Church leaders will be able to see the gaps in their leadership. For example, a pastor may realize the need for more quality accounting practices regarding the church finances. A pastor may go out into the community to see if there are people qualified to help with this need. A pastor may notice the church building needs upgrades and may find a contractor within the community who could help guide the church through this process of renovation. A good leader can lead others around him as well as put the right people in the right place at the right time to implement a plan.[4]

The Need to Be Godly Servant Leaders

The revitalization of the church depends on the revitalization of the people within the church. A pastor needs to realize that patience, grace, humility, and forgiveness will be necessary to lead well.[5] The path to church revitalization is not a straight line. There will be resistance, betrayal, lying, and mean-spirited words and actions. Godly servant leaders do not succumb to depression or lashing out when these come. Godly servant leaders have developed a plan for personal wellness that is able to allow them to withstand these realities without overreacting to them. A pastor in the church-revitalization process who can stay with the plan but out of the fray will emerge with greater respect. Many church members are unaware of the deep dynamics within the church. A new leadership situation gives opportunity for old church

4   Aubrey Malphurs, *Leading Leaders: Empowering Church Boards for Ministry Excellence* (Grand Rapids: Baker Books, 2005), 11–22.
5   Henri Nouwen, *In the Name of Jesus: Reflections on Christian Leadership* (New York: Crossroad, 1989), 71–94.

dramas to play out. However, if the leadership gets pulled into these dramas, they will likely be labeled by the watching congregation as part of the problem. If the leadership can stay above the fray, then the church may come to realize the other, deeper dynamics that have been in play in the church for many years. Often senior leadership can see these moments of conflict as the failure of the plan. However, it is often through these moments of conflict that the church realigns its leadership structure to be able to implement the plan. Senior leadership must vow that no matter how ungodly they may be treated, there will never be a time for the leadership to act in an ungodly way.[6]

STAFF

Pastors of smaller churches often desire more staff to lessen the load of ministry. However, many pastors of larger churches are often frustrated with staff turnover and the difficulty of staff management. Having a quality staff can certainly be an aid in executing quality ministry. However, in church-revitalization situations staff must not only see the vision for church revitalization but also be willing to make the necessary changes to the way they operate their ministries to coordinate with the new realities of church revitalization. It is surprising to some ministers that the staff are as reluctant to change the way they do ministry as the church at large. Staff within churches know how to perform ministry a certain way. A church revitalization calls them to realign the way they do ministry. This requires relearning, rethinking, and fresh planning in ministry areas. Staff may be eager to participate in revitalization or resistant to relearning how to operate their ministry.

Getting the Staff on Board

If the staff are not part of the senior leadership team of the church, it is important that they nevertheless have input into the church-revitalization discussions. Staff, like the church at large, need to be guided

---

6   Robert Greenleaf, *Servant Leadership: A Journey into the Nature of Legitimate Power and Greatness* (New York: Paulist, 1977), 231–61.

through this process. It is unwise to merely inform the staff of the plan and expect them to enthusiastically engage the process. They may not have the skill set to shape the larger plan for church revitalization, but they should be able to give input into the implementation of church revitalization that is most pertinent to their area.

For example, a worship pastor may not need to help craft the churchwide strategy for church revitalization but will certainly need to give input into how the church-revitalization initiative will affect the music ministry. This is especially true if a change of music style is part of this initiative. The worship pastor will know what is doable and will be able to assess the ability of the current musicians and vocalists to execute certain musical styles. Further, the worship pastor could also be aware of the limitations of his own skill set. It would be unwise to avoid working through these realities before implementation. Church leadership will need to embrace the reality that in many aspects current church staff influences the shape of ministry. There is a spectrum of possibilities for ministry among each staff member. It is unwise to task a staff member with an aspect of ministry that is outside the scope of his or her ability and the ability of the volunteers around them. Church leadership must set the framework of church revitalization and collaborate with staff to make sure the expectations are reasonable and the training is adequate for appropriate implementation of church-revitalization initiatives.

Offering Quality Staff Meetings and Retreats

Church revitalization is a process, not an event. A church-revitalization initiative can begin with intentionality and lose momentum and organization after a few months. Many churches repeatedly start new initiatives only to abandon them after a short season of implementation. The cadence of a quality staff meeting can be a weekly, biweekly, or even monthly rallying point to maintain the process of church revitalization. Large tasks must be broken into smaller ones. The ability of church leadership to guide the process of revitalization especially among the staff is critical to positive implementation of church revitalization.

Quality agendas, timelines, meeting preparation, and execution of staff meetings enable clarity in the church-revitalization process. Preparation before a meeting is a crucial factor in the outcome of the meeting. The staff meeting should not be the place where work is primarily started, but where it is discussed and executed. It is important to require each staff member to attend staff meeting ready to present on their ministry area and how they are implementing the church-revitalization initiatives within their area. The staff should not be given a passive role in staff meetings but understand that they are expected to participate. A quality agenda should be sent out ahead of the meeting with clear meeting expectations. While topics can be raised that are outside the scope of the agenda, these need to be placed at the end of the meeting if time allows. This will encourage staff to recommend agenda items prior to the meeting. Accountability to tasks and timelines are important to guide the process of church revitalization. It is important to state what tasks are going to be accomplished and within what timeline. If church leaders fail to maintain this level of clarity, tasks can remain undone for months and stall the church-revitalization process.[7] The staff meeting needs to maintain a professional tone and clearly focus on moving agenda items forward that are consistent with the larger plan of church revitalization.

Developing a Positive Staff Culture

Church revitalization is an arduous process for the staff. The resistance of the church toward revitalization initiatives will initially be felt by the staff in various ministry areas. The staff will be dealing with resistant church members while they are trying to relearn fresh ways for doing ministry. In this context, senior leadership needs to make sure that the process of church revitalization is not all work and no play.

A simple way to maintain a positive staff culture is to create time for staff fellowship that is not work-related. This could simply be done with a bimonthly or quarterly lunch or dinner where the staff

---

7   Patrick Lencioni, *The Advantage: Why Organizational Health Trumps Everything Else in Business* (San Francisco: Jossey-Bass, 2012), 73–188.

is gathered to eat together and fellowship with one another. It is important that this is not experienced by the staff as one more meeting. It could be helpful to invite spouses, select nice places to eat, and avoid church work as the topic of conversation. Also, simple gestures of remembering staff birthdays and work anniversaries and making space in the church office for quality social interaction, in addition to work, make a significant impact.

Since ministry staff are compensated for their work at the church, if the church-revitalization initiatives are successful, it is an important gesture to increase compensation as warranted. A church may be reluctant to offer a raise because of the ongoing financial obligation but could consider a one-time bonus. Also, if there are stressful seasons of new initiatives then additional vacation time could be offered as an act of appreciation. Leadership in a church needs not only to manage the church revitalization process but also to be a pastor to the staff. It is not good leadership if staff leave due to burnout. A reasonable pace must be set to achieve church revitalization while creating a healthy environment for the staff.

Dealing with Reluctant Staff

Good leadership will be able to identify reluctance among staff and address it positively. There are many church stories about staff members who create a great deal of church conflict because they disagreed with the church leadership. These are painful and unfortunate situations. Leadership needs to identify and address reluctant staff early in the church-revitalization process. Resistance to church revitalization falls into several categories. For instance, staff disagree with or do not believe in the church-revitalization plan; staff do not want to learn the new competencies required to execute the church-revitalization plan; or staff cannot learn the new competencies required to execute the church-revitalization plan.

A staff member who does not agree with or does not believe in the church-revitalization plan needs to be seriously heard. It is possible that a staff member could come to believe in the plan after greater clarification, or that they could point out a major deficiency in the plan that needs to be addressed. It is not wise to quickly conclude that a staff member is not "on the team." Simple listening, patience, training, and resources could make it possible for a staff member to champion the church-revitalization plan.

A staff member could be reluctant to learn the new competencies to implement the church-revitalization plan. One of the most important aspects of helpful staff in a church is their attitude. An attitude to learn, grow, and develop is key, as is an attitude to be open to innovative ideas without defensiveness. However, many staff are defensive of their ministry area and desire to do their ministry in a certain way. One simple suggestion is to be willing to take criticism for the staff member if new initiatives in their ministry area are attempted and do not work. Staff are protective of their jobs and do not want to fail. So, leadership support in the new initiatives, especially when the staff are practicing new skills, is important.

A staff member may not be able to learn the new competencies required to execute the church-revitalization plan. While overall a staff member may not be able to do all that is required in his or her ministry area, some aspect of the expectation can be accomplished. This is where leadership can be creative to obtain outside support, volunteer help, or even additional training. The questions that church leadership must ask are: What is reasonable for the staff member to do long term? Can this staff person grow into this position? Can this staff person grow into another position? A staff member who has a cheerful outlook and wants to engage in the life of the church should be given an opportunity to serve according to his or her competencies, even if the person is initially unable to completely fulfill the objectives in their area.[8]

There are situations where a staff member is not on board with the church-revitalization plan. This conclusion should be reached not after weeks but after months of gracious, serious conversations. If it is concluded that the vision of the church and the vision of the staff

---

8   Patrick Lencioni, *Five Dysfunctions of a Team: A Leadership Fable* (San Francisco: Jossey-Bass, 2002), 185–220.

member cannot be aligned, then the path to a gracious departure is important. Leadership and the staff member in question ought to come to terms about their disagreement and develop a plan to move forward. It will not be helpful to the staff member or the church if a staff member is pushed out of a church in haste. A methodical plan needs to be worked out that gives the staff member time to think through family realities, financial issues, and new job opportunities while maintaining professionalism in the current context. Church leadership can ally with the staff member to enable a successful transition for both the staff member and the church at large. Even if this situation becomes contentious, the church leadership can state the process they utilize in staff management, which is founded on doing the best for the church while attempting to be gracious to all staff.

Realigning Staff
Staff within the church must be aligned with the plan for church revitalization. Church revitalization often requires staff realignment. This may mean simply devoting more time to a certain aspect of their job and less time to another. However, the realignment may be more dramatic. A staff member who is currently responsible for youth ministry alone may need to transition into an oversight role for both youth and children's ministry. A staff member who is focused on Sunday school may need to develop off-site groups. It will be important to get maximum effort precisely at the places of ministry that are important to the success of church revitalization.

A hard reality of church revitalization is often that when church revitalization is successful, staff who were able to function well in a smaller, simpler church struggle to adapt to a larger, more complex church. Leadership will have to face up to the reality that a staff member may not possess the level of leadership necessary to conduct the same position as the church becomes more vitalized. Some staff can grow into positions, and other staff struggle to do so. Therefore, it will be important to understand the capacity of each staff member and monitor their ability to adjust if the church revitalization initiatives are successful. If a staff member can grow into a position of greater responsibility, then the church can continue to move forward. If a staff member cannot grow into a new position of leadership, then it will be important to place that staff member in a position that is consistent with his or her leadership capacity.

Recruiting Staff

As a church grows and develops, more staff will be necessary to sustain the church-revitalization effort. Church leadership should always be on the lookout for potential staff. While positions in church are important to define, the right staff member is what makes the position successful or not. Leadership should anticipate the next staff hires that will be necessary if church revitalization occurs. It can be helpful to sketch out a preliminary job description and discuss the plan for recruitment. It is ideal to have a clear job description in hand before actively recruiting for a new position. So much effort can be placed into gaining momentum in church revitalization that little thought is given to sustaining momentum, which often requires hiring additional staff.

DEACONS

The deacon ministry should operate as the ministry catalyst of the church. For church revitalization to occur, the church needs to see the basic ministries of mercy operative in the life of the church. The average person thinks that a church operating properly should rightly care for the poor, the needy, the forgotten, the widow, and the orphan. Sadly, in many churches these ministries of mercy are not as evident as they should be. A robust ministry of mercy through the deacon ministry can galvanize the church to greater service.

The Scope of Deacon Ministry

The New Testament makes a distinction between the role of pastor and deacon. The deacon does not have a leading and teaching function, but rather has the function of ministry. Deacon ministry should not be focused on the organization, planning, and oversight of the whole church but rather on organizing, planning, and executing ministries of mercy within the church. If the deacon ministry becomes encumbered in the oversight of the church, inevitably the ministries of mercy are cut short. It is important to allow pastoral leadership or elder leadership to lead the church and deacons to function in roles of ministries of mercy.

Fueling the Ministry Catalyst of the Church
The unleashing of mercy ministries can hold an incredibly positive effect on the church. While it may be hard to get the church to agree on a difficult change within church structure or church programming, it is uncommon to find resistance within the church when the focus is on taking better care of widows within the church. Often the church needs the presence of a robust deacon ministry to remind the church of the nature of church ministry. The outward call to merciful service to others serves as a corrective to the inward nature of some church programming and personal preference. The call of the church to join with the deacons in these practical mercy ministries can do a great deal in encouraging deepening Christian maturity and ministry within the church.[9]

Specific Tasks, Timelines, and Accountability
Just like the early church overlooked the ministry to the widows (Acts 6:1), so too practical ministry can be overlooked. The deacon ministry is to be aware of the very people the world can easily overlook. Church leadership needs to make sure that the very ones for whom the church should be caring receive appropriate care. Many churches have well-run programs for those who are visible and assertive in the church while forgetting about the shut-ins, the sick, and the widowed. Church leadership needs to define the ministries of mercy that will occur. It is helpful for a singular deacon to take the lead on making sure that ministry is well executed in a particular area. Church leadership needs to set goals even within the deacon ministry. For example, if the church

---

9   Matt Smethurst, *Deacons: How They Serve and Strengthen the Church* (Wheaton, IL: Crossway, 2021).

has a visitation ministry to shut-ins, then clarity on how frequent visits will occur to these shut-ins must be communicated. The sad reality is that if the church is not intentional about performing ministries of mercy, then other obligations will crowd out the church calendar and the very ones who need to be the focus of ministry will be overlooked.

FINDING THE RIGHT PEOPLE AND LETTING THEM LEAD

The church needs to unleash not only pastors and deacons but the entire body of Christ for greater service to him. The goal of church organization is an unleashed church that fits together and works together under Christ the head (1 Cor. 12:12–27). Unity within diversity is the beautiful picture of the church. It is the responsibility of church leadership to aid in this fitting-together process. Church leadership should be personally asking people to lead and aid in the discovery of spiritual gifts within the church.

Finding People with a Certain Skill Set

A functioning church has many skills at work at the same time. For example, a team that can operate a sound system is often necessary for a quality worship service. There is also a need for greeters to extend a welcoming presence to people when they arrive on campus. A strong social media and web presence are necessary for a church to operate in the digital world. A church should also have someone who understands the basics of church safety to operate in a world of heightened safety protocols. These positions do not neatly fall into areas of pastoral or diaconal responsibility. Church leadership should attempt to find people within the church who possess unique skill sets that can be used in church initiatives to move the mission of the church forward.

Finding People Who Lead Well in Other Areas of the Church

Staff may need to be realigned as church-revitalization progresses. Likewise, there may be people within the church who are leading well in one area but have greater capacity for leadership in other areas. God may have already provided leadership. These leaders may just be in the wrong position for this season of their life and the life of the church. Church leadership should contemplate the leadership potential within the church and then evaluate whether they are truly using these people to their fullest potential.

Finding People Who Lead Well in Their Life or Vocation
A church that needs church revitalization has not provided a large enough vision to motivate the church to participate in it. There are many leaders on the sideline as a church becomes less vital. Some members may continue to attend the church out of a sense of commitment or obligation but cease to lead within the church. Church leadership should look around at disengaged people within the church and see if they lead well in their life or their vocation. If a person has a strong family or is capable within their vocation, this reveals that the person can carry the load of leadership but is not doing so within the church. Church leadership will need to provide a compelling enough vision to get sidelined leaders reengaged.[10] This process of reengagement or initial engagement not only may be helpful for church revitalization but may serve as a major turning point in the life of a person who now has a reason to participate more intentionally in the life of the local church.

THE NECESSITY OF A REPRESENTATIVE GROUP WITHIN THE CONGREGATION
Each church congregation is made of groups that socialize together. If a church has one hundred people in attendance, it is often divided into eight or more social groups. This does not mean that the church is divided or dysfunctional, although this could be the case. In any social gathering there are those with whom one develops closer ties. Rather than attempting to address every single person in the church,

---

10   Aubrey Malphus and Will Mancini, *Building Leaders: Blueprints for Developing Leadership at Every Level of Your Church* (Grand Rapids: Zondervan, 2004), 105–238.

church leadership should seek to identify five to eight influential members and communicate with them. This communication can then filter through the congregation to the various groups within it. In some instances, these influential members are already serving as part of the leadership of the church. However, since this is often not the case, it is important to identify, communicate, and listen to this important group.

The Need for Champions of Vision Outside the Leadership Team

While every member should be ministering in a church, not all members have the same level of leadership. Some lead in the church and others follow. No matter how strong a leader is, the leader does not possess the perspective of a follower. A leader must be focused on seeing the plan for church revitalization at a higher level than a person merely responsible for one aspect of the plan or merely attempting to operate within a new structure. Therefore, church leadership needs those within the church who are operating along with other members within a new structure to champion the new structure. If enthusiasm for the church-revitalization plan can be expressed not only by leadership but also by those operating within the new plan, the chances for success are much greater.

The Need for a Representative Sample of the Church to Help Lead

There are always more details to implementing a plan than most leadership teams realize. Many church members who are in a church that needs to be revitalized have become very accustomed to the church experience being a certain way. The smallest change for some church members can throw them into confusion and complaint. While this needs to be addressed as a spiritual problem with the congregant, the timelines of church revitalization will likely not be able to wait until a person who has been ill-tempered for decades transforms into a more temperate person. The more natural reality is that someone will have to help them along in their confusion and complaint. A representative sample of people within the church who can help a leadership team understand where these realities may occur and offer solutions is helpful. For example, the simplest change in some churches must be aggressively managed so as not to stop the process of church revitalization. The changing of the placement of the offering, the order of the worship service, and the location of the coffee pot are trivial in God's great kingdom work but are the very areas that then cause consternation if not anticipated and managed. A representative sample within the church can give the leadership team feedback and insight to avoid making a simple change without understanding the possible full ramifications.

COMMUNICATION AND FEEDBACK

Depending on the polity of the church, the congregation has varying levels of authority. Even in a church structure where the decision-making is confined to a leadership team, the congregation will always have their say. While the church does not operate solely on the leadership team's decisions, it is important to develop a spirit of participation and teamwork. If lines between the leadership of the church and the congregation become too defined, then the congregation can become overly passive. The leadership should call the church to action for the implementation of the revitalization plan.

Allowing for Feedback

There should be opportunities for the congregation to provide feedback to church leadership. If church leadership maintains the right posture, much of this feedback can happen informally. Listening to how the church is understanding the plan is vital for its success. Leadership that is unable to listen carefully to the congregation through the process demonstrates a weakness in leadership ability. There are moments when the leadership team realizes that the implementation of the plan is having trouble. In these moments, a competent leadership team gets out among the congregation, listens to their concerns, and crafts solutions to the problems. The feedback loop from the congregation to the leadership should be continuous throughout the church-revitalization process.

When to Obtain Formal Feedback (or When to Vote)

There are moments before a plan is implemented or after an initial attempted change when it may be important to get more formal feedback from the church. Formal feedback obtained correctly can truly allow the whole church to be part of the development and implementation of the plan. A quality team will struggle to lead if most of the church is simply not on board.

A competent team may simply poll the church on an idea to see how many are in favor or not in favor of the plan. If the leadership team decides to poll the church, the purpose of the poll should be clearly stated and the questions well written. Further, the leadership team should realize that, even in an informal poll, if the poll comes back negative this will require the team to take a novel approach to issues at hand. Other times, it may be necessary to bring an issue to a congregational vote. Once this occurs, the results of the vote can overrule the leadership team. A competent leadership team will rarely bring an idea to a congregational vote without a clear idea of the outcome. Leadership should be among the congregation listening to the church. Informal and formal feedback from the church provides the church with a sense of ownership in decision-making and enables them to be part of the larger team.

PUTTING CONSTRAINTS OF TIME AND TASK ON A TEAM

Teams are temporary constructions. People are put together in a certain organization for a certain season to accomplish certain tasks. Even in churches that have great stability, there is more turnover and change than the majority see. In many congregations, the age of some of the members merely does not allow them to do as much as they did in years past. It is important to have the right team, at the right time, for the right task. In the church-revitalization process, it is vital that teams avoid stagnation.

Setting Clear Timelines and Tasks for Team Structure

Church leadership should know its job. Every person on the leadership team at every level should know their responsible function within the church. Vagueness in job description hinders proper execution of the plan. It is also important that tasks are given an appropriate timeline. Open-ended assignments create a barrier to urgency. Church leadership should clarify what can be attempted even when the job description has some ambiguity and an uncertain timeline. For example, tasking a team leader with the job of evangelism is very open-ended. However, the team leader could set a goal to encourage fifty gospel conversations a week within the church. Then the team leader could report whether this is happening. If it is not, then attempts can be made to adjust the plan or expectation and relaunch the idea. This type of clarity of task and timeline keeps the church-revitalization process moving.

Rotation or Reaffirmation?

A leadership team that helps in one season may not be the right team in another season. A pastor should not assume that the team in year one will be the same team at year five. While it is important to have a level of consistency among leadership, there needs to be freshness on the leadership team as well. Many churches employ a rotation for leadership, limiting a member's stay on the leadership team for a certain amount of time, typically three to five years. The person must step back from their position and reenter after a season away from the position. While this process can sideline good leadership merely for the sake of the system, it serves as an easy protocol to keep the leadership fresh. Another way, which is more difficult emotionally for churches, is to do a reaffirmation. This would mean that after a certain period, some type of reaffirmation process would be completed. If the leader has demonstrated exceptional skill, then the leadership team would affirm his continuation. If the leaders have not demonstrated exceptional skill, then the leadership team would need to express the need for fresh leadership. In churches, the ability to frankly evaluate leadership is more difficult. Thus, many churches opt for a rotation protocol due to its ease of application.

UNLEASHING A QUALITY TEAM

A quality team makes church revitalization possible and enjoyable. A group of people that works together for the renewal of a church is exhilarating to experience. A pastor should not attempt to execute church revitalization without a team. However, once the various leadership members are assigned the various positions, the job descriptions clarified and timelines set, the team needs to be free to operate. The team will not accomplish everything perfectly. The desire to correct, micromanage, or overstep one's authority will be a temptation. However, the team has be set free to operate to see what fresh things God is doing through this group of people at this moment in time. An unleashed team in operation can bring about freshness, vitality, and momentum that the church has not experienced in numerous years!

CHAPTER 8

EXECUTION, EXECUTION, EXECUTION

The time of planning must end, and the time of executing the plan must arrive. Simply put, many pastors assess for too long and execute plans too slowly. Church leadership that stays in the process of plan development too long will hinder the execution of the plan. Planning does not take near the courage of executing a plan. Some churches in need of revitalization have met in committees for years, sharing ideas and making plans with limited execution. Therefore, a cultural shift in the church to move from mere plan-making to plan implementation is necessary for church revitalization. While it is unwise to move too rashly, the needed pace of change in a church revitalization is rather brisk. Even attempting to execute two or three major initiatives in one year takes a lot of time and effort.

PROCEED BOLDLY

What many pastors find especially difficult is that the execution of a church-revitalization plan takes place in addition to the other responsibilities of pastoral ministry. Messages must still be preached, visits made, funerals conducted, weddings administered, church programs managed, and staff supervised. Church leadership must make the decision to go boldly with plan implementation.[1] In any new plan, there are blind spots, weak strategy, and unintended consequences. However, church leadership must make the decision to move and must do so boldly with appropriate confidence and faith in God.

Clarity for Execution		
Task	Timeline	Team Leader
A specific task(s) that will be accomplished	A clear timeline when the task(s) will start, well-defined steps toward goals, and completion deadlines	A well-defined leader who has a well-organized team around him or her

Set a Date and Timeline for Execution

It is important that a plan operates according to a timeline. Set a start date with a clear timeline of tasks to be completed. The team needs to be on the same page regarding when the plan starts, and every team member needs to be able to articulate the action items they are responsible for in the plan. A good team leader needs to ask each team member to state the start date of the plan and verbally articulate their responsibility in plan execution. A lack of clarity and precision in executing a plan will hinder the plan from the beginning. If team members are not able to clearly verbalize the plan and their responsibility, then the team is likely not ready to execute it.

---

1   Peter F. Drucker, *The Effective Executive: The Definitive Guide to Getting the Right Things Done* (New York: HarperCollins, 1967), 1–51.

When executing a plan, both a good start time and a clear plan for sustainability are important. Typically, September and February are good times in the church year to start new plans. September is likely the best time to start a plan because school has begun, and the parents of children are assimilated into a routine. Starting in September provides a full school cycle for implementation. It is ideal to give a plan the most run room possible before a major interruption such as summer vacation occurs. Each church is somewhat different, but every leadership team should know the seasons of church life where the church is more scattered and less focused on participating in something new.

If plans cannot be implemented by September, then February is the next best option. After the Christmas holidays, people need a few weeks to recover from this season. In many places in the country, winter is at its worst in January. However, by February, many have been able to recover from the holidays and are looking forward to spring. The time from February until Easter is a suitable time to start a new initiative, but plans need to be made to adjust the plan during the summer months so that the plan can be reengaged in full in the fall.

The execution of a plan is not merely in starting the plan but in sustaining the plan. Therefore, church leadership should put energy not just into launching the plan but into focusing on how the plan will be sustained in its execution. Sustained execution will focus on pace, having ample staff and volunteers to carry the plan out, and maintaining the team's mindset on sustaining, not merely starting the plan. Plans often begin to show visible signs of working about the time that the team is ready to slow down. Constant encouragement, reiteration of tasks, and emotional strength to press forward are essential to proper execution of church initiatives.[2]

---

2   Chris McChesney, Sean Covey, and Jim Huling, *The 4 Discipline of Execution: Achieving Your Wildly Important Goals* (New York: Simon & Schuster, 2012), 23–104.

Ready the Team

Mike Tyson famously said, "Everybody has a plan until they get hit for the first time."[3] Church leadership must ready the team for the execution of the plan. Conflict is going to arise. Someone on the team will be insulted by a longtime church member. There will likely be a nasty comment directed at a pastor's wife concerning a pastor. A good friend may leave because of disagreements about the direction of the church. Someone may decide to stay in the church and act in a very ungodly way toward a team member. To prepare the team for execution, these potential realities need to be addressed. The team needs to make a commitment that if these unfortunate actions occur there is a predetermined response on how to address these issues as a team. If a team member attempts to take on a church member individually, then this will likely result in irreparable conflict. Further, if there is no plan of action for addressing the difficult emotional realities of plan execution, then it will only take a matter of weeks in some churches for the entire team to fall apart, due not to a poor plan but to a lack of awareness of the emotional angst that would befall them when the execution of a plan began.[4] Further, a wise team leader is going to acquire verbal buy-in that a team member will not undermine the plan to another church member during execution. If a team member sees a potential flaw in the plan, then it is reasonable to address this with the team, so that the team can make an adjustment. However, team members must commit not to collapse under the pressure of church conflict. Again, all team members need to make a commitment to godliness and courage when attempting to move a church toward revitalization.

---

3   Associated Press, "Biggs Has Plans for Tyson," *Oroville Mercury-Register*, August 19, 1987, 1B.
4   Travis Bradberry and Jean Greaves, *Emotional Intelligence 2.0* (San Diego: TalentSmart, 2009), 97–134.

Stay the Course (for a While)

While it is wrong to stick with a bad plan, it is also wrong to fail to stay the course on a plan that has been devised for a set time. One of the tools that team members can use when communicating to the church at large is giving the church a timeline for evaluation. If a new plan is implemented in September, then a team member could communicate that he or she will execute this plan until the end of the calendar year, before making a strong determination of its effectiveness or lack thereof. The communication of these appropriate times for assessment maintains the team's focus solely on plan execution for several months at a time.

Often, a new initiative is started and within a few weeks there is a group of church members who begin to talk and form a group to express their complaints. The team should certainly be willing to hear these concerns and even take notes regarding good observations, but the team must also communicate to the church the desire to try this plan for a certain period before it is evaluated or slowed. Again, team members can be overwhelmed by the emotional responses that occur in churches over the smallest change to church life. Church leadership should state up front that even with all the awareness of the emotional realities of church change, many on the team will still be amazed at the sinful words and actions that will be expressed in the context of a church. The expression of sinful conduct toward team members is one of the profound reasons that the team ought to be committed to see a new plan enacted so that the church can reach a better place of spiritual health. If a team gives up too soon and wrongly capitulates to critics, it may briefly satisfy a critical group but will lead the church to move toward greater decline and death. Like a marathon runner heading into his final miles, there will be many times the team will want to quit. However, a successful team will continue to be resilient and persevere to see real change occur.

MANAGE EMOTIONS

Pastoral ministry does not merely require intellectual competency. It also requires emotional maturity. Implementing change requires more than knowing what needs to be done. Implementing change requires walking a church through a change process. Further, church leaders cannot force people to change. The only thing that church leaders can do is set a context in which change can occur. Creating a change-positive culture can be met with resistance. Church leadership must know how to manage resistance, keep their own emotions in check, and humbly, graciously encourage spiritual health in a church.

Allow People to Grieve (Without Stopping Their Grief)

Not all pain is bad. Some pastors have a fervent desire to keep everyone around them happy. A distressed church member is a sign that something is wrong, which needs pastoral comfort. While in some situations pastoral comfort is good and proper, in other situations sitting with a church member in pain without attempting to resolve it is also proper. For example, when a person loses a loved one, a profound change has happened in that person's life. A pastor should aid in helping this church member accept the new reality of a life without a loved one and encourage the church member to embrace the new season of life. Encouraging a church member to embrace a new season of life without a loved one is by no means diminishing the loss or the joys of a past season.

Similarly, churches have seasons. The joys and successes of a past era should not be diminished; however, neither should a church attempt to relive its past in a new season. The difficulty for many church members is to realize that what was appropriate and contextual in a past era is no longer the best approach in this season. As changes are implemented to encourage church revitalization, church leadership needs to learn how to be sensitive to members' grief without the need to resolve it. A simple strategy requires balancing two realities. One requirement is acknowledgment that stopping a program, changing an aspect of worship, and embracing a different style of church life feels like an aspect of church life is dying away. Church leadership should be willing to celebrate what was accomplished in a past era and be able to understand why it is difficult to see that era pass. However, the same as with a grieving person, church leadership needs to point to the possibilities of this new season, the new joys, the new celebrations they could experience because the church is embracing the realities of this moment. Church leadership must provide space for people to be human and go through natural emotions.[5] If they can maintain sensitivity to the real emotions of people while managing confident resolve in a plan toward spiritual vitality, not only might a plan be implemented but the church members will feel the leadership genuinely shepherding them through the process.

Allow People to Go

Change is just too difficult for some people. Church members must have a certain maturity and readiness to walk through a change process. A person who is under much stress with many obligations may distance from a church while a change process is being worked through. This does not mean that the church member will never come back, but it does mean that walking through change is too much for them right now. Here again, creating gracious departures and allowing people to distance while keeping an open door for their return is important.

Many people may have emotional upheavals but are able to regain composure and work with leadership through a change process. It is important that if someone is experiencing emotional upheaval not to write that person off as a lost cause. However, if after genuine, honest conversations, real sensitivity from church leadership, and even attempts at compromise the church member is still in high conflict, then it is probably best to release them. When the church-revitalization plan is implemented the church that emerges may not be the type of church this person wants to attend. While ideally a particular church can be for everyone, sadly, the highly preferential American society requires certain features of church method and message to be a certain way for them to attend. While this may not be spiritual maturity, it

---

5   William Bridges, *Managing Transitions: Making the Most of Change* (Boston: Da Capo, 2016).

is an experiential reality, and everybody is not going to like the same type of church. Therefore, after genuinely bearing with one another, if departure is the outcome, be gracious, be loving, be discreet, do not get involved in conflict, and leave an open door to the person. Even if their exit is done in ungodliness, this is an occasion for Christian love and grace to be demonstrated.

There is one more caveat regarding letting people go. There are rare occasions that church leadership needs to ask someone to change their behavior or leave the church. Unfortunately, some church members use their positions in the church to bully other members or as a platform for ungodliness. Church discipline is rarely used in the contemporary American church, but it is prescribed in the Bible to faithfully address those within the church who do not desire to follow the commands of Jesus (Matt. 18:15–20). If church leadership decides that this is the only way forward for a church member and the overall health of the church, wisdom in execution will be needed. This will be a painful process even if done with Christian grace and wisdom. However, if this unfortunate situation is present, then church leadership will have to do the challenging thing to bring the church to health.

Dealing with Personal Grief

Church leadership will deal with their own grief through the process. Those within the church are hopefully friends and companions. Church leadership will voluntarily submit these friends and companions to the stress of change. During this process, church leaders will grieve the difficulty of the process. Further, if a good friend who is a church member questions the church leadership, this will also hurt. And if a good friend leaves the church and a pastor loses a close companion, this will engender grief. It might be tempting to stop the change process because the pain of change is becoming too difficult and costly. It is easy in some church contexts to do what a certain group of church members want. Therefore, it is important that leaders give themselves space to be human and grieve the difficult aspects of the process.

When church leaders have a blowup with another church member during the change process, it is typically because they have not appropriately dealt with their own emotions and grief. The need for a support system outside the church is important. Leaders need to be able to debrief with a trusted friend or counselor who is not in the church and can provide an outside perspective, not on the health of the church but on the health of the church leader. Generally, pastors seek help for their own emotional and spiritual health too late, after a church blowup. Sadly, in this situation a pastor must recover from the disruption of the trauma of the church blowup along with addressing unprocessed grief that preceded this moment. Therefore, a clear plan for addressing the emotional and spiritual health of church leadership needs to be in place before a change process is begun.

Adjusting to New Realities

As new realities of the change process emerge, they can become obstacles to execution. Church leadership often has a vision of how the change will be when it comes, but typically it is not exactly the way they expect. Further, church leaders who were able to lead in one context may struggle to find their way in a new context. Some of the leaders who were able to execute through the change process will no longer be able to lead once the change is in place. There is an adjustment period, not only for the church but for the church leaders. The norming of new realities in a church is a vulnerable time. In some ways, the new realities will be good and helpful, and in other ways they will be deficient. It is important that church leaders not focus on what is going wrong but on what is going right. A pastor must learn to be a different type of pastor in a new context, a deacon must learn to be a different type of deacon in a new context, and a ministry leader must learn how to lead ministry in a different way.[6] It is not merely the process of

---

6   John Maxwell, *5 Levels of Leadership: Proven Steps to Maximize Your Potential* (New York: Center Street, 2011), 21–36.

executing change that is difficult but also the process of settling into new realities. This can be an exciting and celebratory time full of mixed emotions, but church leaders who are able to implement changes like this keep pressing on in the context of change and adjustment to new norms.

MANAGE EXPECTATIONS

During the change process, church leadership needs to manage expectations for the church. The decline of the church took years to materialize, so the revitalization of the church will also take time to develop. If a church can grow very quickly due to a few interventions, then the church can also decline very quickly if those interventions begin to fail. The goal is to produce solid, stable growth that can be maintained over time. Just like a person who is attempting to save money or lose weight, initial interventions do not make a person get in great shape or become financially stable. However, if proper interventions are maintained over time, then health will emerge. This is as true in the life of a church as in any area in life. A change in the overall patterns of a church over a sustained period produces health. There are no quick fixes, and church leadership will need to manage expectations that change will likely produce gradual health, not explosive growth.

Play Up the Benefit (Restate the Why)

While the plan for church revitalization is being implemented, the why must be constantly restated. Much time and energy will be focused on the actual implementation of the plan. Church leadership will consist of realigned staff and ministry leaders, launching programs, managing the calendar, and overseeing the budget, all in the context of a church that is attempting to adjust to new realities. Church leadership must constantly restate why the church is putting itself through this change process.[7]

---

7   Simon Sinek, *Start with Why: How Great Leaders Inspire Everyone to Take Action* (New York: Penguin, 2009), 133–74.

Church leadership will need to frequently restate the desire for the church to thrive into a new generation, the vision of raising up new leaders to reach a new generation, the hope that the future days of the church will be greater than any past era, and the aspiration that the work of past generations will be the foundation on which a robust ministry presence will remain in the community into the future. The why should be very personal. To an older generation that has labored in the church, leadership needs to state the why this church will be a place where their grandchildren and great-grandchildren will serve and minister. People must know the reason behind the action. The smaller the why, the less the motivation to endure. The bigger the why, the greater the motivation for the congregation to push forward through turbulent emotions to achieve a goal that is compelling enough for the present discomfort. Church leadership must not only lead but also cheerlead. It is not enough to merely develop a plan. The constant championing of the plan and the why for plan implementation is necessary to maintain momentum and encouragement within the church.

Downplay Notions of a Silver Bullet

There is no one intervention that will bring a church to spiritual health. This idea must be combated. While church leadership will need to do one thing at a time, it will be the cumulative effort of many interventions that encourages health, not just one change. It can be difficult in the execution process when an intervention is successfully implemented. A win is gained, but many problems persist. Church leadership needs to wisely point out that this singular intervention brought about an area of greater health, but other interventions will be required to encourage health in other areas.

Church leadership will need to incrementally execute tasks to bring the church to greater health. This incremental approach toward health is often slower than most want it to be and not nearly as flashy as some would hope. However, church leadership again needs to tell the church how each incremental step brings the church one step closer toward health and must be careful not to overpromise what one change will do. Further, church leadership will need to state why a single intervention does not result in revitalization. Many within the community have either no direct contact with the church or had an unpleasant experience with the church. It is not reasonable to conclude that one act of kindness to the community will reverse years of inaction or overturn an unpleasant experience. For a church to win the community, it will take a sustained barrage of ministry to overturn the perception of church inaction or past hurts. It will only be after the church has truly reached a level of spiritual health that the community will begin to believe the church might be different.

CELEBRATE WINS

Execution is an event and a process. Tasks are executed, but the execution of a plan takes time and intentionality. It is important to celebrate wins along the way. The church needs clarity that revitalization takes time, but it also needs to see progress toward the goal. Therefore, it is important to garner short-term wins that are consistent with the long-term goal of the church. Depending on the situation, it is often important to front-load the church-revitalization plan with several short-term wins to build momentum and grow confidence in the church toward the prospect of revitalization.

Identify Early Wins and Communicate Them

A plan to communicate successes needs to be in place. It can be easy for church leadership to become so focused on executing the plan that wins fail to be communicated. The weekly gathering for worship is an excellent time to take a portion of the church service to celebrate what God has done this week in the life of the church. The cadence of celebration sets a new culture of expectation and enthusiasm that is contagious. Communicating wins to the church enables the church to see in tangible ways that God is working.

The task of identifying wins should not belong to church leadership alone. The church should be unleashed to identify the ways that God is working. There needs to be a communicated protocol in place so that wins are recorded and communicated in an appropriate fashion. However, church leadership ought to recruit some key leaders in the church to show how the efforts of revitalization are occurring in various ministry areas. Pausing to celebrate what God is doing further propels the church into greater ministry. However, failing to appreciate and celebrate what God is doing will likely slow momentum because the church will become weary.

Develop Routine Appreciation

Church members must be appreciated for their efforts in revitalization. Part of celebrating wins is celebrating those who have worked hard for them. If a ministry team has implemented a major task toward revitalization, this effort must be appreciated by the church leadership. This could be as simple as a complimentary email, handwritten note, or phone call. It could be as elaborate as a celebration meal. It is important from time to time to stop and have a celebration. Taking a ministry team out to dinner or having a special celebration as part of a worship service goes a long way to encouraging the church. Many church members are willing to work extremely hard for the ministry of the church if they believe their effort is seen and acknowledged along the way. The process of change should not become so burdensome that only a few resilient leaders are able to weather it but rather should maintain a cadence of hard work and celebration. This cadence can make the process of change not only doable but in many respects enjoyable.

THE IMPORTANCE OF SMALL WINS

Church leaders must understand that change is a process to be managed and the power of a win is important. Some pastors want to front-load their church-revitalization plan with many difficult action items—fully rewriting the constitution and bylaws, purging the church rolls of inactive members, and starting a capital campaign to raise money for building needs. Starting a church-revitalization plan with this many difficult objectives may make sense strategically but will not likely make sense to a church emotionally. If everything the church does is very hard with few clear results, the plan may fail. The need to mix hard tasks with a few easier tasks is important.[8] Again, each church situation is unique. But rarely is a church that needs revitalization ready to take on only tasks that are emotionally difficult without easier tasks to offset them.

Growing in Leadership Credibility

Church leadership typically has less credibility on the front end and earns credibility as the plan begins to be executed successfully. More than one thing is happening at one time. Church leadership may simply think that their job is to implement a church-revitalization strategy. However, their job is to demonstrate competency early in the process so that the church can trust them with greater decision-making power as the process continues. Leadership sometimes inverts this reality. They assume that, because they have already received authority to execute initiatives, they do not need to manage the congregation's perception of their actions. Church leadership should assume that they begin the implementation with little trust from the congregation and that this trust grows only as initial interventions are successfully implemented, with tangible results that the church is able to celebrate. They are not merely attempting to implement a plan but are attempting to demonstrate competency and credibility through the change process.

Building Momentum

Church leadership can see the entire process of revitalization and should diligently communicate it to the church. However, the church experiences the process of revitalization week to week and month to month. If the initial changes in church revitalization do not go well, the willingness of the congregation to continue in the process can diminish. There is a level of pain that each church is willing to endure. Some churches are willing to make a series of very hard decisions and endure acute pain to see church revitalization

---

8   Charles Duhigg, *The Power of Habit: Why We Do What We Do in Life and Business* (New York: Random House, 2014), 31–96.

occur. However, many churches are not willing to endure as much pain on the front end.

Building momentum through the acquisitions of early wins is needed in most churches. Many churches are willing to endure a mixture of hard changes and positive changes on the front end. All the essential changes will not be made within the first six months or year. Church leadership ought not be disheartened but be aware of how earlier wins are developing momentum in the church for more interventions. If momentum builds, ideas that would have cost a great deal of strife in the congregation may be met with far less resistance. As wins are acquired, more members begin to believe in the church-revitalization plan and grow in confidence in the church's leadership. Momentum is a powerful thing, and managing momentum is important. Church leadership needs to balance the needs of the church now with the long-term strategy for church revitalization. If initiatives are implemented that destroy the momentum of the church, then likely this intervention will hinder any future changes to occur for a significant period. So, church leadership will need to evaluate the importance of the initiative and its effect on the overall momentum of the church.

ADMIT WEAKNESSES
(WITH POTENTIAL SOLUTIONS)

No plan is perfect. No leaders are perfect. There will be aspects of the church-revitalization plan that will not work as expected. This is not necessarily a failure of planning but the limited nature of human strategy. Humility is a trait of a good Christian leader. Godly church leaders will be willing to state when things do not go as expected and are willing to be appropriately self-critical when necessary. A church will struggle to develop trust in church leadership that hides from its flaws. While it is important to be optimistic about the church-revitalization plan, it is bad to be defensive and elusive when things do not go well. Church leadership will need to be able to state the rationale for the plan, the unexpected realities that altered the course of the plan, and how they learned through the process. If the church begins to feel that church leadership is not being transparent and honest, credibility will be lost.

The Humility of a Postmortem

There need to be scheduled postmortems for evaluation. While a church-revitalization plan may be five years in length, these plans have initiatives that are completed at varying times. It is important to do a significant postmortem every six months, if not every quarter. Postmortems give church leadership the opportunity to reflect on the successes and weaknesses of the past. Church leadership can typically discern whether the previous quarter in church life was generally positive or negative. It is difficult to sustain church revitalization if more than one quarter of a church year is negative. Like a sports team that is playing a four-quarter game, church leadership needs to keep a pulse on whether the initiatives in the past quarter were generally positive or negative. If church leadership suffers a difficult church quarter, then they will need to look for ways to make sure in the upcoming quarter that interventions are seen in a more positive light. The skills to assess the past while planning the present are essential to continuing church revitalization.[9] Therefore, church leadership should not just push ahead without taking some time to evaluate past interventions.

Stating What Could Have Been Done Better (but Not Too Early in the Process)

Execution of tasks will require both humility and resolve. There will typically be a church leader who wants to reevaluate the plan too early in the process. This is typically because they are not emotionally ready for the execution process. At the first sight of pain, they are ready to abandon the process to make sure everyone is happy. This is a recipe for making no one happy. So, church leaders should not

---

9   Chari Smith, *Nonprofit Program Evaluation Made Simple: Get Your Data, Show Your Impacts, Improve Your Programs* (Portland, OR: Author Brick Road, 2020), 9–50.

undermine the church-revitalization plan while it is in the initial process of implementation. There should be at a minimum three months of execution before the plan is reassessed. If a plan requires major revisions after the first three months of execution, then the failure is not in the execution but in the writing of the plan. A well-devised plan should not have much unexpected resistance within the first six months.

Church leadership can communicate to the congregation early in the process their desire to evaluate the plan, but for this period the focus will be on truly attempting to implement the plan. It is advisable to state that there will be a formal evaluation of the plan in three months, six months, or whatever the determined time frame is for initial execution. There will likely be some church members who will want to sabotage the plan from the inception. Church leadership will likely need to continue to implement the plan while these church members complain.

It is important that when a formal evaluation is done the facts establish a strong baseline for analysis. For example, if a goal of the church-revitalization plan was to grow attendance in small groups over a six-month period, then hard data could prove whether this occurred. Something that may come as a surprise to some church leaders is the failure for some in the congregation to believe hard data. If some within the church do not want the church to change, they will even object to hard data if it is not in their favor. Reports made to the congregation should thus be very meticulous. This is best done through writing an executive summary of effects of the church initiatives with a supplement that shows hard data. This way those who object to the summary can reference the supplement. The desire for church leadership is to give an objective report of the strengths and weaknesses of the interventions and not allow speculation and opinions of those with a desire to resist change to paint a false picture. Church leadership will need to state confidently what worked and why, and to honestly state what did not work and how going forward church leadership will address it. The church must see the church leadership as more objective and honest than those who resist change.

EFFECTIVE, STEADY, RESILIENT EXECUTION

Plans only affect change when implemented. Plan implementation takes as much grit as knowledge. For a church to see real change happen, church leaders will need to be bold, humble, focused, open-minded, honest, and resilient. Developing a plan is not sufficient for church revitalization. The day-to-day perseverance to see incremental tasks accomplished in the context of praise and criticism is what is necessary for real change to occur. Church leaders must commit to pressing on when they are hurt and tired.[10] This change process will test church leaders' resolve. Even though this task may not be enjoyable in the moment, leading a change process is a profound opportunity to develop in spiritual maturity, learn deeper compassion, rely on Jesus with greater intensity, and trust God for the vitality of his church!

---

10   Robert Dee, *Resilient Warriors* (San Diego: Creative Team, 2011), 37–56; and Gary Moritz, *Carry On: Tactical Strategies for Church Revitalization and Renewal* (Orlando: Renovate, 2021), 86–102.

CHAPTER 9

MANAGING CONFLICT, MAKING PEACE

F ollowers of Jesus are called to be peacemakers (Matt. 5:9). However, to bring about true peace sometimes conflict must be engaged. The balance between real peace and conflict is complex. Change often brings conflict. Old structures are remade so that new realities can be experienced. Since change is a process, not an event, church leadership must monitor the entire process so that conflict does not destroy the opportunity for change. One way to prohibit change is for the conflict intensity to become so great that the change process is abandoned. Therefore, in the context of implementing change, leaders must offer careful attention given to the level of conflict experienced in the church. Competent leaders are neither willing to allow the status quo to remain, nor are they willing to allow the process of change to become unmanageable.[1] Striking this balance requires skill and awareness of those within the church.

---

1   Ken Sande, *The Peacemaker: A Biblical Guide to Resolving Personal Conflict* (Grand Rapids: Baker Books, 2004), 21–74.

Monitoring Conflict

Church leaders cannot abandon implementing change at the first sign of discomfort. However, neither can they ignore conflict when it begins to become acute. There is a middle ground between discomfort and acute pain. If the church is not moving through change quickly enough, those who are ready for implementation will become discouraged. If the church implements change so quickly that it is emotionally overwhelming for some, members may distance themselves or leave. A mass exodus during a change process is not ideal. In many situations, there is a group that will distance or leave during change. However, if this group becomes too large, the level of conflict can halt the change process. Church leadership must monitor the level of conflict during the change process.

Why Things Cannot Get out of Control

Church leaders must commit to ensure conflict never gets out of control. Moments when church members begin shouting at one another or someone has a tearful, angry moment as part of a meeting can traumatize the church. If these moments of intensity are allowed to escalate, they will greatly hinder the change process. While many church members are willing to experience discomfort, few are willing to hang around if a situation begins to get out of control.

Church leaders do not have ultimate control over whether someone chooses to have an angry outburst or a tearful moment. However, they must attempt to work toward prevention of such moments and have a clear plan of action if these moments occur. Prevention of out-of-control moments relies heavily on the church leaders' knowledge of the congregation. Some members are more short-fused or emotional. It is important during church gatherings to merely observe such people in a meeting. Typically, there are a host of nonverbal cues displayed before a person has an outburst. A church leader can watch for these cues. If they become present, a church leader could merely go and sit next to the person. Further, if a church member has a history of outbursts in church meetings, a one-on-one discussion with the person before the meeting to address concerns might be in order. If a church leader believes that a meeting is set to be an explosive environment, it would be unwise to conduct the meeting in the same manner as planned. It would be ideal to reduce the group size and especially address the most explosive members in private. The damage of allowing a large-scale conflict to occur in the presence of other church members will cause the congregation to lose confidence in the church leadership's ability to enact change.

There are situations that can surprise church leaders even with the best planning. If unfortunately a large-scale conflict does occur, church leaders must minimize damage. The best thing to do if emotional escalation occurs is to immediately turn attention to bringing emotions and tempers back in order. The discussion at hand should immediately stop and the person running the meeting should call for order and godliness. The church leaders will need to be calm and authoritative in this moment. If the person is unwilling to calm down and committed to making a scene, the meeting should be adjourned, and the people dismissed. It is unwise to allow church members to continue exposure to a volatile church environment. Once this has occurred there will be a significant amount of repair required. Church leadership will need to follow up with each person involved, express their regret for the development of the volatile situation, and reaffirm their commitment to a peaceful environment. When a situation has gone bad in a church, some members never recover, some members blame the church leadership for allowing it to happen, some blame the person who got upset in the meeting, or some combination of these factors. It is never ideal for the focus of the church to be on the conflict within the church versus the implementation of a plan toward church revitalization.

MAKING PEACE

While conflict must be managed, it also must be engaged. And in remaking systems of behavior that will move the church toward health, conflict and resistance are a necessary reality. Church leaders will not be able to see church health emerge without some level of conflict.

Making Peace Is Different from Keeping the Peace

Making peace requires upsetting the status quo so that a better reality is maintainable, understanding the role of conflict in the change process, and discernment of the places where the church has learned to accept less than ideal situations.[2] Many families clearly know the difference in keeping peace versus making peace. In most family units there are certain family members who do not treat other family members with the love and respect they are due. The family merely has learned how to live with these people. They allow injurious behavior to continue because the family has decided it is easier to keep peace than make peace.

Making peace would require lovingly but firmly addressing the family member and no longer accepting certain behaviors. This is a complicated process, and many families (and churches) have chosen to merely keep peace versus making peace. While in the short term it certainly does feel more comfortable to keep the peace, the long-term consequences in families (and churches) to merely keep peace versus making real peace are dire. If a situation remains broken long enough, those who have injurious behavior usually become more emboldened in their behavior. Those who tolerate the behavior become less aware of its effects on the church family and even in their own lives. A church that wants to see real change take place must move from a mindset of keeping peace to making peace.

Conflict Is Necessary to Make Peace

The church must discern the places where they have accepted a less than ideal situation. There could be groups within the church that spar with one another. There could be staff who refuse to be accountable. There could be deacons who use their position to bully others. The church has decided when they merely keep the peace in these situations that this reality is acceptable. If church leadership is willing to state that these realities are not acceptable, then the tiring process of precisely addressing these areas to make real peace is necessary. Addressing the long-standing patterns of behavior will bring about some level of conflict. This form of conflict must be engaged and managed for genuine peacemaking to occur. Without conflict there will be no real peace in broken situations.

---

2   Jim Van Yperen, *Making Peace: A Guide to Overcoming Church Conflict* (Chicago: Moody, 2002), 163–75.

Conflict is the path to real peace and vitality. If through a conflict process bad behaviors are addressed and removed from the church environment, church members can inhabit a healthier environment with real peace.

AVOID GETTING INVOLVED IN CONFLICT

Church leadership must possess genuine spiritual and emotional maturity to bring about appropriate conflict in the church without becoming involved in conflict. Addressing challenging situations to make peace requires resolutely avoiding becoming enmeshed personally in the conflict. If leadership is seen by the church as fighting a personal battle or engaging in a personality conflict, then they will lose the respect needed to enact change.

Avoid Taking Conflict Personally

The church will react to change. Members may say hurtful things to those in leadership. Even if these attacks are personal, or feel personal, church leadership cannot take these actions and words personally. This is much easier said than done. Removing personal feelings from the conflict can allow others within the congregation the possibility to see their own behavior. The way it typically works in other relationships is someone loses their temper or manipulates a situation to get their way. The other person typically meets anger with anger or gives in to the manipulation. Those who are mean-spirited or manipulative in a church context have been given a long time to practice within their own network of friends and family. It is very surprising to these people when behaviors that get a response in another context do not work with a leader in the church. Positively, if a pastor is willing to help people like this see their behavior and lovingly redirect it to a more appropriate end, it could help them address deep behavioral and spiritual issues. For this to be accomplished church leadership must both stand in the fray to enact change but also stand outside the fray when it comes to being too personally impassioned.

Emotional Resoluteness in Conflict

It is hard to overstate the emotional drain that church conflict can cause. The simplest of tasks can feel like an impossible obstacle in light of certain personalities and anticipated conflict. It is precisely at this point that all pastors and church leaders must have a plan for their own personal wellness and spiritual health. Church leadership will not be able to walk through these seasons of conflict without deep spiritual resources sustaining them. It will be easy for church leadership to walk away from the conflict or merely stay in a broken situation with a lack of desire for change. They must develop emotional resoluteness in the face of conflict,[3] understand that appropriate conflict is necessary for real change and peace within a church and believe that it is worth the momentary struggle for a renewed revitalization in the church.

Boundaries and Grace

Church leadership must continue to love their congregation through the conflict while also being real about their own humanity. It is important that church leadership not get angry or emotional during church conflict. Boundaries and grace are required. For example, a pastor may need to realize that he will be unable on Monday morning to address a certain church member after a long Sunday. This will require him to establish certain boundaries.[4] It only takes one bad interaction with a church member to set the change process back. Church members can express behavior in unbecoming ways on a regular basis. However, if church leadership has one bad moment, church members will remember and recall it often. Therefore, leaders should recognize the moments when they are too tired to address certain church members or situations.

Church leadership must also learn to manage the congregation with grace. The truth is that all who are resistant to change and demonstrate poor behaviors in the process of change believe they are fighting for worthy causes. The cause may not be worthwhile at all,

---

3   Daryl R. Conner, *Managing at the Speed of Change: How Resilient Mangers Succeed and Prosper Where Others Fail* (New York: Random House, 2006), 224–66.

4   Henry Cloud and John Townsend, *Boundaries: When to Say Yes, How to Say No to Take Control Of Your Life* (Grand Rapids: Zondervan, 2017), 165–208.

but the person fighting for it believes the cause is just, whether that cause is preserving some aspect of church life, keeping things as they remember in a former time, or anything else. These beliefs motivate the person to continue to press their cause. Church leadership with a pastoral heart ought to at least be able to empathize with their cause even if they disagree with their rationale. Even though the person is doing harm to the church, church leadership should deal with them in grace. If a person genuinely believes that church leadership is dealing with them gracefully even in opposition, it could win them over.

CHARTING THE CONFLICT

Church conflict is not the result of one or two persons. It is a group effort. Even those who sit on the sidelines and allow poor behavior to be perpetuated have played a role in keeping the drama alive. A church should not think that the removal of one or two people will change the entire system. While the absence of a few people within a church may certainly reduce conflict, it certainly will not bring a church to health. A revitalized church will need to address long-standing patterns of thought and behavior that are in the vast majority of members. There must be a change of church culture, not just the removal of a few of the loudest and most belligerent.

The Church as a Family System

Humans live in networks of relationships. A church is a system of relationships. There are rules of engagement when a person enters a certain church. Every person who enters a church operates within preset systems. Many within a church feel about the church systems as they do about their own family systems. Writing a history of the church typically reveals the patterns of behavior that affect congregational life (see chap. 3).[5] Short pastoral tenures, limited outreach, poor decision-making, and so forth are symptoms of deeper structural realities. Church leadership should evaluate the

---

5   R. Robert Creech, *Family Systems and Congregational Life: A Map for Ministry* (Grand Rapids: Baker Books, 2019), 3–30.

reasons why less than ideal behaviors not merely have been perpetuated in one season of the church but are repeated throughout
many seasons. It is common for churches to complain about a
former pastor and subsequently hire a new pastor that has many
of the same personality traits. This behavior gives evidence of a
deeply rooted church pattern. But a simple review of the church's
history from another vantage point would reveal these certainly
visible patterns. Once these patterns are seen, the church can work
together to see why they exist and what can be done to address
them. However, for church patterns to change everyone must
play a different role, which will require change that some will be
reluctant to make.

How All the Church Allows Repeated Patterns to Continue

The church needs to be willing to take responsibility for its history
and its present reality. If old problems or conflicts are being repeated
in the present, it is the priority of the entire church to evaluate what
role each individual church member is playing in this drama. This
can include bullying, passivity, enjoyment of drama, minimization
of conflict, and so forth. No one within the church is free from
contributing to the context that has made the church what it is.
While some have more prominent roles in the life of church, the call
for everyone to assess their contribution to the problem can enable
true transformation to take place. If church leadership addresses the
family system of a church outside the conflict, then church leaders
can highlight the presence of old patterns reemerging in the present.
Hopefully, armed with new data on why these dramas keep repeating
themselves and the roles played by all within the congregation, the
hope for deep transformation can become reality.

It is important that church leadership sit down and draw out
a diagram of the conflict. Who is involved in the conflict? Who
has grouped together? Who is grouping around key leaders? What
is the nature of the problems? What is the disagreement between
groups? Is the disagreement focused on church leadership or somewhere else?

IDENTIFYING PROBLEM-SPOTTERS, PROBLEM-STARTERS, PROBLEM-STIRRERS, PROBLEM-SOLVERS, AND PROBLEM-SNOOZERS

It is important to understand the various roles that those within the church play when problems arise. There are several types of reactions. Drawing out the conflict on a whiteboard or large sheet of paper can enable a more accurate understanding of things.[6] It is important to church leadership to have some understanding that not everyone is responding in the same way. It is easy to hear about a problem only from one person or one group and lack awareness of the larger network of relationships involved in the conflict.

Charting Conflict

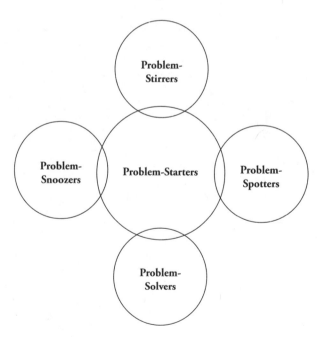

---

6   Monica McGoldrick, Randy Gerson, and Sueli Petry, *Genograms: Assessment and Interventions*, 4th ed. (New York: W. W. Norton, 2020), 35–193.

Problem-Spotters

There is a group of people within most churches who want the church to be free from conflict. If there is anyone who has hurt feelings, they typically inform the church leadership that someone is upset and needs to be addressed. These are problem-spotters. In some ways, their job is noble. They typically have a compassionate heart; they want to see people in the church receive ministry and keep an ear to the ground for potential conflict. Problem-spotters can inform church leadership of problems before they grow into large conflict and for this reason can play a good role within the church. Problem-spotters, however, often fail to make peace where the goal is to keep peace. They can be most keenly aware of the people within the church who express the greatest discontent. These problem-spotters see it as their mission to make sure that church leadership knows about every problem they hear about. It can be hard to communicate to those who want to keep peace with everyone that some discontentment within the church will be necessary to move a new plan forward. The problem-spotter will typically fail to be receptive to this concept because the concept of making real peace versus merely keeping the peace is not their typical way of approaching the situation. The problem-spotter is often fixated on the person expressing the problem without a wider view of the situation.

Problem-Starters

Problem-starters are neither all good nor bad. Some church members will perceive church leadership that implements new practices within the church as problem creators. It is important to note the nature of the problem in question. Would addressing this problem bring about the health of the church? If the focus is addressing a good issue in an appropriate way, then these types of problem-starters can play a helpful function. For example, if a deacon decides that he is going to attempt to implement a policy that holds the deacons accountable for the ministry they are responsible to execute, then that is a positive initiative when executed with firmness and grace. The main difference between good and bad problem-starters is the motivation and the nature of the change.

Many ill-intentioned problem-starters have their own interests and desires at heart, or the interests and desires of a particular group rather than the whole church. This type of person will create a lot of commotion if changes in the church do not appease them or their group. Further, if the nature of the problem raised focuses on the needs of a particular group to the exclusion of the needs of the church, then these types of problem-starters can hinder church revitalization. There is often a particular group within a church that has limited desire to be missional and a powerful desire to keep things in the church that appease their needs and their routine. If church-revitalization changes threaten these needs in any way, many within this group will become very antagonistic to church leadership. Church leadership needs to remember that if the true purpose of these problem-starters is merely to maintain the status quo, when the status quo is reasserted this group will have virtually no desire to reach outside their group to expand the ministry of the church. This group may give lip service missional endeavors, but often the long-term objective historically is to maintain programs and routines that minister to them and have little to show in genuine outreach. If church leadership does not appropriately address this group in grace and keep momentum toward real church change, then this group will bring the church back to the same state in which it has cycled for decades.

There is no reason to demonize problem-starters. They have often seen pastors come into the church and implement change poorly and may genuinely believe that the changes being implemented will not work. When church life looks different from past experiences this group may have a challenging time seeing it as progress. It is also possible that they are not aware of the obstacles to change they are creating. What is even more difficult is that those who do have awareness adopt a very passive-aggressive attitude. Church leadership must be ready for those who will create problems to protect and maintain their group and the ministries dear to them. Capitulating to groups like these will keep the church in stagnation, but dealing incorrectly with them will provoke conflict in the church. It will take wisdom, skill, patience, and intentionality to negotiate situations like this well.

Problem-Stirrers

Problem-stirrers are quick to jump on the bandwagon of those voicing problems. This group has various motivations for joining in with those who are concerned about the direction of the church. Some can be more easily influenced by their situation and quickly ally with someone who is voicing an alternative position. Some have family situations that are in constant turmoil, and this family dynamic spills over into the life of the church. Others attempt to elevate their own status by standing for a cause within the church. Problem-stirrers often do not have all the facts concerning a situation and sometimes lose interest in stirring the problem as quickly as they gained interest. Problem-stirrers move from one grievance to the next throughout the church and their own lives. Church leaders can best address problem-stirrers by isolating one-on-one with them. Typically, problem-stirrers find solidarity within the group. If a church leader graciously reaches out to them, problem-stirrers are typically willing to back down. Often a church leader's acknowledgment and concern regarding a problem is sufficient to provide confidence to transition to another area of interest.

Problem-Solvers

Problem-solvers are those who are willing not only to address problems within the church but also to do the challenging work of developing and implementing solutions. A large majority of these should be in some position of leadership in the church. If a church has strong leaders in various positions, problems are addressed and resolved in an efficient and peaceful manner. Problem-solvers are not necessarily those within the church who make no waves. Especially in a church that needs revitalization, someone will have to state the problems that have led to stagnation and develop and implement solutions to reverse decline.

Church leadership will need to harness the ability of the problem-solvers in the church. In some church situations, problem-solvers leave because church leadership is not willing to give over sufficient authority for those within the church who could solve problems to do so. It is ideal not only to have top-level problem-solvers within church leadership but also to find problem-solvers and place them in key positions in every critical ministry position. A strategically placed problem-solver in every key position throughout the church will make the job of the church leader much easier. If a ministry area is full of problem-starters, problem-stirrers, or problem-spotters, then church leadership will constantly be called to referee problems in those ministry areas.

Problem-Snoozers

In the most conflict-filled church, there is always a section of the church that is unaware of what is occurring. This group is labeled problem-snoozers and becomes aware of the problem only when the most dramatic actions are taken. The dismissal of a pastor, the cancelation of a ministry, the dramatic cutting of the budget, media publicity brought on a church situation, or other topics of higher magnitude are required to gain their attention. As a problem has exploded or is in the final stages of resolution, there will typically be a group that begins at that time to ask what is happening. Church leadership should not be surprised at how aloof certain sections of the congregation can be. For some, their life is full, their obligations are many, and their time and energy are spent elsewhere. They come to church for a haven and are not inclined to think about organizational realities of church life. The best way to deal with this group is to provide a simple response to the problems facing the church. Typically, a brief explanation is all they desire.

ASSESSING CHURCH STRUCTURE

Church structure can encourage conflict. For example, in some congregational models of church government, the congregation is not only the ultimate authority but also the only authority. The way the congregation wields its authority is through majority voting and complex parliamentary procedure. Scenarios like this set the church up for conflict. Unity is not the goal of such a structure, but only understanding who is in the majority. No group holds authority to lead over any area, only the will of the congregation. An authoritative group typically influences known ways to stop any form of leadership they do not appreciate. In these models, authoritative groups spend much time and energy developing coalitions, gaining the majority, and demoralizing new leaders. Even godly people placed in a very polarized, competitive structure may find it difficult to exercise godliness and grace. The same reality can be true for overly top-down models where authoritarian leaders or church models overrule the voice of the congregation. The structure of the church may be one of the major contributing factors toward conflict. In many church-revitalization situations, church leaders should revise bylaws to create more intuitive, unity-promoting systems to address conflict.

Avoiding Unnecessary Conflict
It is reasonable to ask: How much of our church conflict is based on the church structure? Could the presence of a new or modified structure promote attitudes of real peacemaking? As church leadership charts out the conflict over time, it may become apparent that major conflict occurs in the context of confusing business meetings or dictatorial practices of a certain church leader. If church leaders could put structures in place to change the terms under which the major conflict occurs, it may be possible to mute some of the conflict within the church.

Remaking Structures to Encourage Peace
Church leaders may make a major contribution to peacemaking through church education on contributing structures of conflict. The church could then collaborate to address creative ways to build structures that promote peace. For example, a church that requires 50 percent for a plan to pass could require 60 percent instead. Those who are skilled in getting 50 percent of the church to go along with their program would be encouraged to talk to an additional 10 percent of the church that was previously unengaged. Church members casting negative votes without any rationale may be requested when voting no to submit a written or verbal rationale to church leadership. This would offer a more open discussion of why decisions are consistently

unsupported within the church. Some faced with the prospect of stating their reasons for voting no may just abstain from voting if they believe their rationale to be less than noble. In a church structure where a small group has too much authority, systems of accountability could be developed to provide the congregation ample resources to hold leadership accountable. These changes in structure could encourage members of the congregation to bear with one another rather than competing with one another.[7]

DEVELOPING A GRIEVANCE PROCEDURE

A church should have a grievance procedure to address conflict. If church leaders funnel grievances through an intentional process, then church leaders can save time and energy chasing the problem down from less than assertive members. If a church does not have a grievance procedure, then unnecessary conflict is required to get the leadership's attention so a problem can be addressed. If there is a clear procedure regarding how to hold a hearing concerning a problem, then church leaders can address problems more directly.[8]

Funnel Disagreement Through a Formal Procedure

A formal grievance procedure is as simple as making a box available, having dedicated email for grievances, or listing a phone number where a congregational member can explicitly state a concern. It is especially important that those who receive and manage the grievances be level-headed, good listeners and have wide respect in the church. There must be a sense of impartiality and fairness in addressing each grievance. However, having a single place where grievances are funneled can remove unnecessary disruption in the congregation so that church members do not feel the need to stir up the entire church before church leadership can intentionally address a concern.

---

7   Daryl R. Conner and Mark A. Murphy, *Leading at the Edge of Chaos* (Upper Saddle River, NJ: Prentice Hall, 2002), 240–46.
8   Peter T. Coleman, Morton Deutsch, and Eric C. Marcus, eds., *The Handbook of Conflict Resolution* (San Francisco: Jossey-Bass, 2014), 533–57.

Educate Congregation to Utilize the Process

Often church members will resist utilizing a grievance procedure. Some simply do not like change. However, others desire to avoid giving their concerns in a methodical manner. They want to be able to express their discontent within the wider church to recruit supporters, not to find resolution. If the congregation can be educated to believe in the effectiveness of a grievance policy, then when a certain church member attempts to recruit people to their cause, those people handling grievances can merely direct that person to express that concern through the formal process. Typically, in a church system that does not allow members like this to express discontent in an unbridled way, these types of church members will distance themselves from that church and find one where they can express discontent apart from accountability structures. Again, a good structure can eliminate the platform for ungodly behavior.

ADDRESSING GRIEVANCES

If church members submit grievances in a grievance policy, then the procedure for addressing grievances needs to be credible and efficient. In order for the congregation to have confidence in the process, church leaders must address grievances in a timely, gracious, sensitive, and decisive manner. If the grievance process does not adequately address conflicts, then it will move outward into the life of the church.

Executing Protocols

A grievance policy needs the following components to be effective. First, a grievance policy needs to have a clear and easy avenue for stating a grievance. Church leaders should make this available by providing a box for notes, an email, a phone number, or a designated contact person. Some people prefer to write their grievances, and others prefer to express them verbally. Second, the team of people receiving and responding to the grievances must have reputations of godliness and fairness. Respect for those addressing the grievances will go a long way toward a congregation's accepting a resolution. Third, church leaders must thoroughly understand the expressed grievance.

While it is important that church leaders address grievances in a timely manner, they should listen well and pause for necessary reflection, never giving a rushed response. Fourth, a clear and written resolution that states both the concern and the resolution must be written up and made available for the church to review publicly. Details and personal issues need to remain private, but clarity on the nature of the grievance and the resolution must be publicly available when it is prudent to do so. Fifth, if possible, all parties need to be able to sign off on the resolution. There is a tendency for some in church life to agree to a resolution in one context and then go back on their decision. A formal process binds a person to their word, which discourages and sometimes exposes church members who go back on their word.

Addressing Grievances Face-to-Face

It is important that church leaders address grievances face-to-face. There is a level of civility found in face-to-face discourse that cannot be counted on in written or electronic communication. It is not sufficient to answer an email or make a phone call if someone has expressed a grievance, and it is often important to meet the person who has expressed the grievance initially in a context that is conducive to their own comfort. A church leader could meet the person at their home, or the person could bring a friend to the meeting with church leaders. Face-to-face meetings should be structured, allowing both sides the opportunity to speak so that one side does not possessing an advantage. From the moment a church member submits a grievance, a face-to-face meeting should occur within seven days.

The Need for Understanding the Problem Under the Problem

Emotional intelligence is critical when dealing with church conflict. Often the conflict in one area is related to a host of other interpersonal conflicts and family dramas in the lives of church members. A pastor can be an easy scapegoat when life is not going as a person thinks it should. When a person is unsettled with God it is easy to transfer that blame to the person who serves God in full-time ministry. Therefore, the presenting issue is rarely the main issue. Sometimes a person wants to be heard, cared for, or feel respected by a leader within the church. This does not mean that the presenting issue should not be given sincere consideration. However, church leaders should be on the lookout for another issue under the stated issue. What makes this more problematic is that church members are often unaware that there is another issue under the stated issue. Church leaders must deal with these issues sensitively. Revealing to a person that their issue might be rooted in a deeper personal issue could unleash personal pain that the person has not dealt with. If the person addressing the issue does not proceed with gentleness, they could easily create an emotional blowup. Dealing with underlying issues can be emotionally tiring; however, rooting out deep-seated conflict and interpersonal complexities is a part of real church revitalization and genuine personal renewal for church members. Church leaders should see these moments as opportunities for deep discipleship rather than being disheartened by the difficulty of these moments.[9]

Limiting Emotional Energy on Those Who Seek Only Conflict

Some church members repeatedly seek conflict. While one should avoid writing people off too quickly by assuming this is the case, if after two or three genuine attempts at reconciliation the behavior begins to be remarkably similar and conflict rages on, it is likely that the person is seeking only conflict. In such cases it is important to limit emotional energy spent on the problem. Often this type of person desires to maintain a position of control in their family and in the life of the church. Therefore, conflict is brewing everywhere if this kind of person cannot have their own way. Sadly, a person with this outlook only appears to be content in a church situation when everything is going their way. As soon as anything appears to go counter to their desires, they respond with blatant belligerence or deception. This is a clear case where keeping peace cannot be confused with making peace. With a person who only participates in one-way compromise,

---

9   William Ury and Bruce Patton, *Getting to Yes: Negotiating Agreement without Giving In* (New York: Penguin, 2011), 15–94.

the appearance of peace is merely giving in to their demands. It is important for church leaders to avoid becoming bogged-down dealing with high-conflict people. Graciously address the person several times, and if it becomes apparent that this is a high-conflict person, then continue to implement the plan, be gracious to the person, and do not allow the anger or deception they express to change the course of action.

Writing It Up and Taking Good Notes

Church members can agree one moment and change their minds the next. The need for a formal conflict-resolution process should include good notetaking throughout the process and a final written statement of compromise at the end. Many people do not know what they think about a given issue and then change their mind on the issue depending on the circumstance. A church member can sit and discuss an issue and come to some resolution only to leave the meeting and reverse course. Further, in the presence of church leadership some church members will not express their true feelings. They will wait until they are in the presence of good friends and then let their true feelings be known. Often church leadership will learn through the church body about a complaint from a person who seemed to be in agreement during a conversation. Therefore, written notes, verbal affirmation, and compromises must be documented. This is invaluable. When a complaint arises, church leadership can state that a written compromise was agreeable to the involved parties on a particular date. Again, this is an opportunity for discipleship. If it is common for a person to change positions, complain in private, and then hide from real conflict resolution, this pattern can be addressed. Their practice affects not just the life of the church but many areas in the person's life.

The Need for Patience and Taking a Break for Reflection

Conflict resolution is an emotional process. Emotions need to be expressed, but it is unhelpful when they get out of control. Therefore, doing enough to process emotions and work through issues, but not doing too much to crash the process is important. Further, the life of the church cannot be solely about addressing conflict. It is important to set a reasonable cadence of conflict and taking breaks. Church leaders cannot ignore problems long term; neither can long-term conflicts be addressed in a month. Therefore, church leaders will need to stay attuned to when church members involved in conflict need a break. Sometimes taking a week off from addressing a problem can enable the parties to reach a resolution sooner than driving through the conflict without breaks. Sometimes people just need a break to stop, reflect, and recover before they are willing to come to a resolution. There must be a time to come back together and readdress the issue. So, when the parties take a break, it is important to agree on a timeframe for resuming the conversation.

Coming to a Resolution

Church leaders must not pass over the possible for the perfect. A compromise is rarely the ideal. A compromise is the blending of multiple perspectives that develops an outcome where few get everything that they want, but all get enough to stay with the group. In church life, church leaders will have to live with less-than-ideal resolutions or be willing to lose a group within the church that is unwilling to embrace the changes proposed. After three to six months of deliberation over a conflict, the options for resolution should be present. None of the options may be ideal, but after a process has been engaged, it is important to develop the best resolution possible and then move on. Changes in churches are often incremental. If major change is implemented and the church body is not ready for it, then it is likely that the church body will reject the church leadership, and little will be accomplished. Therefore, church leaders must engage the conflict-resolution process with patience, persistence, and willingness to accept the best resolution that is possible at the moment.

A CULTURE OF MAKING PEACE

If church leaders are genuinely open to dialogue, willing to embrace a fair conflict-resolution process, and demonstrate they are open to reach resolutions that keep the congregation together, then a culture of making peace will develop. Church disagreements will no longer be seen as insurmountable obstacles but merely problems that can be addressed through a process. The overall emotional temperature of the church will drop, and the church will grow confident in its leaders and their ability to negotiate the problems that appear along the way. This is an ideal place for a church to be if they are truly going to work toward church revitalization.

The Principles of Humility, Forgiveness, and Reconciliation

Conflict resolution is a wonderful place for deepening discipleship and real renewal to occur. The virtue of humility is so critical for church leaders and church members to possess. Willingness to express one's limits and dependency on God for any good outcomes is critical. Church leaders who have worked hard on a plan for church revitalization should be humble enough to express the possibility they could be wrong and willing to learn from the congregation.

Forgiveness is an extraordinarily complex process. The biblical command to forgive is straightforward (Eph. 4:32). However, the process toward forgiveness is not. A major factor in true forgiveness is the ability of the offended to see the offender in new ways. The statement "forgive and forget" is simply not possible or true. The offended must be able to see the offender with eyes of compassion without justifying the offense. Deep forgiveness requires stating the offense, seeing the offender with newfound compassion, and giving a genuine gift of forgiveness. No one can rush the process, which requires learning the practices of forgiveness. A church that is truly going to heal from past events must learn real forgiveness.

Reconciliation is different from forgiveness. Forgiveness requires one person, while reconciliation requires two people. Reconciliation requires two offended parties to address one another at the same time with humility and grace. Further, the person who has been offended will likely need the offender to make some type of amends. This is an arduous process because any time both are not willing to work together the process is halted. True reconciliation is different from mere tolerance of another person. It is the development of a new relationship that is founded on understanding and forgiveness that is the result of a past conflict. For real and deep healing, church members must move beyond tolerance of others to genuine reconciliation.[10]

MAINTAINING PEACEFUL CONFLICT

Churches do not have to be defined by conflict. Every church has conflict, but healthier churches use the moments of conflict to learn and grow rather than destroying one another. It is not possible to be emotionally immature and spiritually mature. Therefore, poor behavior in conflict raises not only emotional dysregulation but also spiritual issues. As church leaders set the pace and as the congregation is willing to collaborate with one another, a peacemaking culture can be developed. The clearest sign of this developing is that the emotional temperature of the church doesn't skyrocket when a conflict arises. If the church starts leaning into the problem without attacking each other, then a peacemaking culture is developing. If the church treats each problem as an opportunity to move into factions and fight, then work is still needed in developing a peacemaking culture. The solace to church leaders is that few moments will lay people barer, expose deep issues, and possess an opportunity to truly help people change. Rather than being disheartened by conflict, commit to leading the way to true peacemaking—not only renewal of the church but deeper renewal in the life of those within the church. It is important to embrace the role of peacemaker as a faithful disciple of Jesus (Matt. 5:9).

---

10 Everett Worthington Jr., *Forgiving and Reconciling: Bridges to Wholeness and Hope* (Downers Grove, IL: InterVarsity, 2003). Worthington understands the practical realities of attaining real forgiveness and reconciliation and provides an excellent process for attaining them.

CHAPTER 10

WHERE TO GO FROM HERE?

t is hard to know exactly when a church in need of revitalization has been revitalized. Changes are made, progress is measured, but there is always more to do and more people to reach. At some point, typically around year five, church leadership may affirm a church has moved beyond the need for revitalization to a state of revitalization. It is important not to declare victory too early in the process because a series of successful interventions does not mean revitalization has been achieved. Sometimes a few successful interventions are met with delayed resistance or unexpected obstacles. Typically for a church to reach revitalization a church must successfully implement a series of changes, negotiate conflicts, and emerge on the other side of the conflict with the presence of a new church culture emerging.

WORKING ON THE NEXT WAVE OF CHANGE

It is important to celebrate victories along the way. The journey to revitalization requires a reasonable pace and focus. However, as soon as one successful wave of changes has been implemented, a new wave of changes must be developed and implemented. This is in many ways a constant process of planning, implementing, analyzing, adjusting, and executing initiatives. Actually, the process requires church leadership to be thinking ahead even amid the current change.[1] One success often leads to another opportunity or obstacle. Simple realities like growing worship attendance create a parking-space problem or focusing on groups requires additional volunteers in children's ministry. Church leadership must always stay focused on leading and adjusting.

Updating the Plan for the Next Wave of Change
Five- to Ten-Year Year Aspirational Goals
What is the best-case scenario for the church in five to ten years? Develop the vision of what this would look like.
Five-Year Actual Goals
List actual goals that must be accomplished for the aspirational goal to occur over the next five years. Write out goals and action plans. 1. Goal 1 (with a detailed plan of action) 2. Goal 2 (with a detailed plan of action) 3. Goal 3 (with a detailed plan of action) 4. Goal 4 (with a detailed plan of action) attempting in next wave of change 5. Goal 5 (with a detailed plan of action) attempting in next wave of change
One-Year Aspirational Goals
What is the best-case scenario for the church in the upcoming year?
One-Year Actual Goals
List actual goals that must be accomplished for the aspirational goal to occur in the next year. Write out goals and action plans. 1. Goal 1 (assemble leadership team) accomplished ✓ 2. Goal 2 (clean and update building with repairs/paint) accomplished ✓ 3. Goal 3 (develop community outreach event) accomplished ✓ 4. Goal 4 (hold a staff retreat) accomplished ✓ 5. New Goal 1 (with a detailed plan of action) 6. New Goal 2 (with a detailed plan of action)

---

1   Doug Morgan, *If You Will Lead: Enduring Wisdom for 21st-Century Leaders* (Chicago: Agate B2, 2018).

Why This Process Is Repeatable

The same process that began church revitalization can be repeated. Church leadership can perform an assessment of the personalities in the room, the status of the church, and the needs of the community. They can then develop initiatives that can be implemented within a reasonable amount of time (six to eighteen months) and that are consistent with the long-term vision of the church. Church leadership can assess the previous initiatives to determine whether there is more to accomplish and consider new opportunities. One indication that revitalization is emerging is that there is a new rhythm of planning, praying, and executing. The days of meetings without execution, long seasons of indecision, and cumbersome policies are slowly being replaced by more intentional processes.

Why This Process Can Be Compounding

New initiatives on top of new initiatives do more than merely change a few things to enhance the life of the church. A series of changes on top of a series of changes has a compounding effect. For example, enhancing the welcome-team ministry could lead to more greeters at the entrances of the church. However, typically as time passes a series of changes such as better visitor communication, better visitor information capturing, and better follow-up all begin to occur as the church is encouraged in one area. What may have started as merely making sure every visitor is greeted turns into a robust system of visitor outreach and follow-up. Mastering a simple task allows for other tasks to be considered. If this can happen across several areas in the church over several years, what began as a few simple initiatives has developed into multiple complex systems of operation. Church leadership will have to be patient and intentional to see small initiatives grow into larger processes.

Staying Fresh

What worked yesterday may not work today. Strangely, the very leadership that led a church into greater revitalization can halt revitalization in another season. The same problems of rote repetition of past initiatives can easily become the default because these worked in another era. The very patterns that led the church into stagnation are the very patterns that can creep back into church leadership. It is truly tiring to constantly attempt to be fresh, see with fresh eyes, think new thoughts, and push toward new realities, but this is what is required if churches are going to consistently minister to their communities over the long term. People are more transient. The complexion of the church can change from season to season, and the needs of the moment are different.

Church leadership will need to discover ways to make sure that appropriate freshness is maintained season to season, either through rotating leadership, evaluating leadership, or replacing leadership. Further, many volunteer leaders desire to sit back for a season to recover after leading a wave of changes. Some volunteer leaders are unaware of how much emotional energy has been expended until it is time to start another wave of change. Often at that moment, many realize they do not have the emotional energy for another round of implementing changes. Paid leadership too will need to think carefully through their wellness plan to make sure they are ready for another wave of change. It is not wrong to pause from major initiatives for a few months while people recover. Appropriate breaks may be ideal so that everyone is able to stay fresh and motivated as time passes.

The Development of a New Culture

At some point, the old church that was present seems to be gone. One of the joys of church revitalization is staying at a church long enough that it no longer feels like the church it once was. It is a strange phenomenon to be at the same church for several years and feel like it is a different church. This is the essence of real revitalization. A new church culture is developed. New processes are implemented. A fresh spirit fills the worship, and a new enthusiasm motivates the ministry. It is important to celebrate this wonderful moment when it happens. What the church might have deemed as unattainable five years earlier has been obtained. Church leadership ought to take full advantage of these moments. Rehearse what God has allowed the church to accomplish on the church's anniversary each year. When the change is undeniable, the goal obtained, and new realities present, it is clear to everyone that something new has happened and a new, fresh church has emerged from the smoldering ashes of the previous church.

WHAT IF I FAIL?

Church revitalization is not a straight line of successful interventions. Even the best leaders will struggle to discern all the hidden realities that hold the church back until they appear in real time. Setbacks and failures are part of the learning process. It will take time to uncover the various obstacles. Further, it will take time to discover what is acceptable in a particular church or community. This learning process will lead to momentary failure. This failure is not absolute. It is an opportunity to adjust and learn.

You Will Fail

In church revitalization it is important not to be deterred by failure. Embrace the reality of failure as part of the path to successful church revitalization. Failure can be a friend if it is managed properly. It gives an opportunity to analyze why the failure took place. Failure could be the result of the wrong plan, attempting to do too much too soon, a lack of able leadership, hidden resistance, poor timing, not taking care of the spiritual and emotional health of church leaders, or conflict with a person or group within the church. There is no successful leader who does not face failure. The key is to see failure as an opportunity to truly do the challenging work of analyzing it. Learn from the failure, make better plans, see the situation more clearly, and try again.[2] Failure will happen, but failure is never the final word for God's church.

A Firm Identity in Christ Through Failure

Church leadership and especially pastoral leadership must have a firm identity in Christ apart from successes and failures in church

---

2   John Maxwell, *Sometimes You Win, Sometimes You Learn* (Boston: Center Street, 2015).

life. When the success of the church is necessary for the emotional stability of a pastor, then ministry needs to be refocused. If a pastor is too tethered to the success of the ministry, then he will make mistakes in leadership. For example, if a pastor needs the church to be happy with him, then he may move into a chaplain role where he only attempts to meet needs and keep everyone happy. While chaplain care is noble, it can be detrimental to leading the church to health. On the other hand, if a pastor feels he needs to make the church successful, then he may attempt to push an agenda and fail to remain in attunement to the emotional state of the church. The need to succeed at all costs could be the very reason that clever ideas fail. The congregation senses that the success is more for the emotional needs of the pastor than the good of the congregation. Pastoral staff and church leadership should deeply analyze their desires and motivation for change. If church revitalization is truly pursued out of a heart of love for God and his church, then the church will intuitively know this. Developing intimacy with Christ and a firm identity apart from ministry success and failure is critical to being able to gracefully walk the road of church revitalization.[3]

An Opportunity to Be Humble and Learn

The willingness to continually learn and stay humble is critical for a healthy Christian life and is necessary for church leaders. Leaders never arrive. What makes a church leader successful in one place and at one time may not make them successful in another place and another time. While the centrality of gospel proclamation and the ministry of the church are stable over time, people and cultural moments differ. This requires fresh analysis of how best to engage the current church in the current moment. Church leaders should be reading, rethinking, analyzing, dreaming, and learning to be the best they can be. Experience in church revitalization can become a hindrance if through successful experience church leaders fail to realize that church life

---

3   Eugene H. Peterson, *The Pastor: A Memoir* (San Francisco: HarperOne, 2011).

has to continually be freshly analyzed. Further, generational change occurs so rapidly that what is acceptable to a new generation is far different from what reached the last generation.

Church leaders likely need to set up a formal process to keep learning. This may require setting a book list to read, attending conferences, visiting other churches, and meeting consistently with young leaders or older leaders. The process of learning must be intentional because time passes quickly and one's outlook on the current state of church ministry must keep up with the changing realities of the moment. This learning process does not mean that church leaders set aside their convictions. Church leaders need to know what type of church they are attempting to produce. However, with conviction in hand, church leaders must ably address the contemporary moment with wisdom.

A Sign to Move On to a New Assignment?

Church leaders should not leave too soon. It is common for pastors to start looking for an exit plan after the first major conflict. The sad reality is that many pastors who leave during a major conflict in one church end up repeating history in another church. There are many churches in America that share many common problems. Pastors and church leaders must be willing to face the moment. If the problems facing the American church were easy, the problems would already be solved. Difficult problems and conflict may not signal the need to move to a new assignment; they may signal the need to dig deeper into the problems and work toward resolution.

There are situations where failure is the impetus for God to move a pastor on to another place of ministry. It is important to run toward a new ministry, not just run from an old ministry. Pastors need to develop the characteristic of contentment and avoid reacting too quickly. When God has provided clarity for a new assignment, a gracious departure is important. Pastors and church leadership may have a vision for church revitalization that a church rejects. However, typically the rejection is not total. There are typically aspects of the church-revitalization plan with which the church agrees. A pastor who is considering a new assignment in the future could attempt to

execute a few initiatives that the church desires to accomplish as part
of his gracious departure. Leaving well is important. To an already
weakened church, a pastor who leaves in disruption reveals a dearth
of character and does greater harm to the church. If a pastor leaves
a church in a rage, it reveals that he was not mature enough to lead
church revitalization nor is he ready for a new ministry elsewhere.

Success Does Not Equal Avoiding Failure

Success in church revitalization does not equal avoiding failure. It
merely means not quitting after failing. Church leaders must maintain a
reasonable pace, not take themselves too seriously, accept failure as part
of the journey, and joyfully continue. Often failures give church leaders
the opportunity to establish credibility. The ability to fail on a task, be
gracious and humble, learn, and reengage the church is an opportunity
to garner respect. The greatest gains for church revitalization typically
occur further into the process than most desire—usually somewhere
after year five. The short-term tenure of many pastorates and the desire
of some church leaders to see instant change lead many to jettison success because they quit too soon. It is for the faithful, persistent church
leaders who work through failure to see revitalization emerge, not from
a lack of failure but by continuing through failure to success.

HOW TO KEEP REVITALIZATION ALIVE

There is a point at which a church moves from a need for revitalization into a state of vitality. However, continued vision in a church is
necessary to keep it moving forward. As soon as a church fails to have
vision that gives the church direction, the danger of decline emerges.
While past gains can buy the church some time before decline occurs,
the characteristics of vitality need to be present in every season. Some
practical ways to keep vitality are a God-sized vision, bold incremen-
talism, and strategic patience.

God-Sized Vision

It is important to meet goals, but it becomes more difficult when the
church believes that a vision has been achieved. If the vision can be

fulfilled within ten years, it is likely the vision was not large enough. If a church fulfills a vision, then church leaders must cast a larger, more compelling vision. Many churches can fall into the trap of making an attendance number, a building, a budgetary goal too closely aligned with the larger vision of the church. When these realities are attained there is a collective relaxation in the life of the church. Clarity in vision should never be mistaken for a few numbers or a building plan. These realities should be leveraged for greater mission. It is not clear at all that a church that has merely attained a level of financial and attendance success has become vital. Measures such as how many lost are being reached, how much intentional discipleship is happening, what the church's impact on global missions is, and how the church is serving the needs of the community in practical ways are truer signs of spiritual health. It is hard for the church in need of revitalization to see that real, God-sized vision is not merely avoiding closure but being leveraged for greater ministry.

It will be important as the church is emerging out of a state of crisis into a state of vitality to hold forth the mission ahead and not declare a mission accomplished. The church that has moved from the need for revitalization to vitality is now ready to minister in ways that it had not in previous years. Ministering from a place of health and vitality enables a church to truly influence the people within the church and those without the church. Vitality is a healthy place to embrace God's greater mission.

Bold Incrementalism

Once a church has accomplished major tasks that were essential to putting the church on the path to revitalization, smaller changes still need attention. There is always room for improvement in the life of a church. Church leaders need to continually ask, "How can the various ministries of the church be improved?" There should be a culture of excellence and improvement that pervades church life. No ministry area should be content to merely go season to season without improvements.

Slight changes in various ministries can truly make a major difference in the church. Some ministry leaders will make just enough changes during the big push toward revitalization and then stop once the urgency has passed. This is planting seeds of decline. It is important to give the various leaders in the church a break after a long season of revitalization. However, it will be unwise to avoid reengagement. All leaders should be pushed to higher levels of achievement. It may be necessary to require innovative ideas or a new initiative in every ministry area, every year. Incrementally improving the ministries of the church will make substantial changes over time. However, it will require real intentionality by church leaders to make sure that the church is boldly, incrementally changing every moment.

Strategic Patience
New seasons offer new opportunities. Ideas take time to be acceptable. The joy of being at a church for a long season is that ideas that would have been roundly rejected in one season are welcomed in another season. For example, what the church was unwilling to do to reach a section of their community in one season is taken up and realized in another. Just waiting for the right people and the right moment will enable ministry opportunities to present themselves. Strategic patience is a skill set that must be maintained through the church-revitalization process.

Promising ideas do not have to be forgotten; the ideas may just need to be put on hold until the moment is right for implementation. Church leadership needs to understand the importance of timing. Church leaders who can be strategically patient will be able to move a church forward over the long term, while those who lack patience to wait for the right moment will not be as likely to achieve their goals. Every few years the complexion of the church changes, new dynamics emerge, and new possibilities are offered. Executing change when the moment is right is more enjoyable for both the church and the church leadership, but strategic patience is necessary.

HOW MUCH CHANGE?
Change in the church requires change in the church leadership. As a church grows heathier and more vital, the discomfort of change

may be most acute among certain leaders. Some who were able to lead in one era simply cannot grow into the new church reality or choose not to participate. One of the difficulties for church leadership is to watch leaders leave or be asked to leave because they are no longer able to fulfill a leadership role in the church. This moment in particular does not feel like revitalization but is actually very much part of the process. A church will struggle to rise higher than its leaders, and often the church is unable to know how high their leaders can rise until the reality of change and growth occurs. Some leaders will flourish, and others will falter in new environments. Change will pressure leaders to change, so this reality ought to be anticipated.

How Church Change Makes You Change

Church leaders will need to know how to take on new roles as the church changes. For example, it may be necessary to be very direct in the initial stages of church revitalization. It is not uncommon for churches with only one compensated pastor to require the pastor to clean the building, organize the worship service, do office work, visit the sick, and plan the programs. While this might be the reality in one season, it cannot be the reality in future seasons. The question becomes: When the new season emerges, will church leaders and pastors who have been very direct be able to step back, train others, oversee, and lead at a different level? New seasons will require new competencies. Church leaders must be willing to make these changes and lean into this moment. If not, the ones who will be a hindrance to revitalization and unwilling to change will be the church leaders themselves. Pastors will need to think carefully through their skills and abilities and determine what type of leader they are best suited to be. The average-sized church is fewer than two hundred persons. This could be because the average pastor is able to oversee a group of this size and no larger. Clearly, some pastors could grow beyond their current state of leadership. Others may not be able to lead a ministry over a certain size. This is not an admission of failure, but appropriate self-reflection and humility.

Assessing How Much Change You and Your Church Can Handle

Church leadership must assess the following areas. First, how much can this current leadership team change? There must be a realistic assessment of how far the current leadership team can take the church. The gifts and abilities of each person must be assessed, and the goals reviewed. The church may need to gain new leaders to be able to move the church forward. However, the church needs to be on the lookout for new leaders who are willing to be trained. Periodically, the leaders of the church need to be asked whether they have the passion to see the church continue to grow and change. Waning vitality and passion are typically a clear sign that this leader has reached a point where they are no longer interested in leading into a new era.[4]

Second, how much is this church willing to change? After implementing a series of changes and experiencing vitality, a realistic assessment of how much the church wants to continue to change needs to be made. How big of a community and global impact does the church want to have, and how much is it realistic for it to have? How complex does the church want the programs to be? Does the church even want to be a program-based church? To continue to move the church forward, it is important to discern what is reasonable for this church in this location to become.

Third, what are the limitations of the current location and facility? Rural situations are different from urban ones. Poverty-stricken areas are different from affluent ones. While the church is not a building, the building and the community in which is it placed put limitations on what can occur. While these limitations can be overcome, does the church want to relocate? Does the church want to purchase more property? Does the church want to embrace a multisite model? Does the church want to invest in other church plants? Does the church want to adopt other churches in need of revitalization? The physical limitation of space and the economic limitations of a community

---

4   Gary L. McIntosh, *Taking Your Church to the Next Level: What Got You Here Won't Get You There* (Grand Rapids: Baker Books, 2009), 115–80.